Family Enterprise

Understanding Families in Business and Families of Wealth

THE FAMILY FIRM INSTITUTE, INC.

WILEY

Cover image: texture © iStockphoto.com/gaffera; leaves © iStockphoto.com/hugbee
Cover design: Wiley

Copyright © 2014 by The Family Firm Institute, Inc. All rights reserved.

Published by John Wiley & Sons, Inc., Hoboken, New Jersey.
Published simultaneously in Canada.

No part of this publication may be reproduced, stored in a retrieval system, or transmitted in any form or by any means, electronic, mechanical, photocopying, recording, scanning, or otherwise, except as permitted under Section 107 or 108 of the 1976 United States Copyright Act, without either the prior written permission of the Publisher, or authorization through payment of the appropriate per-copy fee to the Copyright Clearance Center, Inc., 222 Rosewood Drive, Danvers, MA 01923, (978) 750-8400, fax (978) 646-8600, or on the Web at www.copyright.com. Requests to the Publisher for permission should be addressed to the Permissions Department, John Wiley & Sons, Inc., 111 River Street, Hoboken, NJ 07030, (201) 748-6011, fax (201) 748-6008, or online at www.wiley.com/go/permissions.

Limit of Liability/Disclaimer of Warranty: While the publisher and author have used their best efforts in preparing this book, they make no representations or warranties with respect to the accuracy or completeness of the contents of this book and specifically disclaim any implied warranties of merchantability or fitness for a particular purpose. No warranty may be created or extended by sales representatives or written sales materials. The advice and strategies contained herein may not be suitable for your situation. You should consult with a professional where appropriate. Neither the publisher nor author shall be liable for any loss of profit or any other commercial damages, including but not limited to special, incidental, consequential, or other damages.

For general information on our other products and services or for technical support, please contact our Customer Care Department within the United States at (800) 762-2974, outside the United States at (317) 572-3993 or fax (317) 572-4002.

Wiley publishes in a variety of print and electronic formats and by print-on-demand. Some material included with standard print versions of this book may not be included in e-books or in print-on-demand. If this book refers to media such as a CD or DVD that is not included in the version you purchased, you may download this material at http://booksupport.wiley.com. For more information about Wiley products, visit www.wiley.com.

Library of Congress Cataloging-in-Publication Data:

  Family enterprise : understanding families in business and families of wealth / The Family Firm Institute, Inc.
     pages cm. — (Wiley finance series)
  Includes index.
ISBN 978-1-118-73092-8 (cloth); ISBN 978-1-118-73098-0 (ePDF);
ISBN 978-1-1187-3091-1 (ePub)
  1. Family-owned business enterprises. I. Family Firm Institute.
  HD62.25.F3765 2014
  338.6–dc23
                                            2013027432

Printed in the United States of America.
10 9 8 7 6 5 4 3 2 1

Family Enterprise

Founded in 1807, John Wiley & Sons is the oldest independent publishing company in the United States. With offices in North America, Europe, Australia, and Asia, Wiley is globally committed to developing and marketing print and electronic products and services for our customers' professional and personal knowledge and understanding.

The Wiley Finance series contains books written specifically for finance and investment professionals as well as sophisticated individual investors and their financial advisors. Book topics range from portfolio management to e-commerce, risk management, financial engineering, valuation, and financial instrument analysis, as well as much more.

For a list of available titles, visit our website at www.WileyFinance.com.

Contents

Acknowledgments ix

**Family Enterprise: Understanding Families
in Business and Families of Wealth** xi

CHAPTER 1
Defining Family Enterprise 1
   Definition 1 2
   Definition 2 2
   Definition 3 2
   Definition 4 2
   Definition 5 2
   Family Business Review article: "From Longevity of Firms to Transgenerational Entrepreneurship of Families: Introducing Family Entrepreneurial Orientation" 4
   Assessment Test 1 37

CHAPTER 2
Classic Systems of a Family Enterprise 39
   The Family System 40
   The Ownership System 41
   The Enterprise System 42
   Assessment Test 2 43

CHAPTER 3
**Representative Governance Systems
in Family Enterprises** 45
   Enterprise Governance 46
   Family Governance: Family Council 48
   Owner Governance: Ownership Forum 49
   Assessment Test 3 50

CHAPTER 4
Key Characteristics of Family Enterprises — 53
- Characteristics — 53
- Challenges — 54
- Comparison of Family Systems and Enterprise Systems — 55
- Assessment Test 4 — 57

CHAPTER 5
Concepts in Family Enterprise Study — 59
- Systems Thinking: A Very Brief History — 59
- Systems Thinking: The Individual in the System — 60
- Relevant Systems Concepts: Triangles, Scapegoat(ing), Homeostasis, Boundaries — 61
- Content and Process — 63
- *Family Business Review* article: "Using the Process/Content Framework: Guidelines for the Content Expert" — 65
- Assessment Test 5 — 77

CHAPTER 6
Theoretical Frameworks in Family Enterprises — 81
- The Three-Circle Model — 83
- The Developmental Model — 87
- The Balance Point Model — 88
- Assessment Test 6 — 89

CHAPTER 7
Core Professions Working With Family Enterprises — 93
- Differing Perceptual Filters — 95
- Understand the Differences Among the Core Professions — 96
- Assessment Test 7 — 99

CHAPTER 8
Multidisciplinary Professional Teams — 101
- Types of Teams — 101
- Challenges Teams Face — 102
- *Family Business Review* article: "The Effects of Goal Orientation and Client Feedback on the Adaptive Behaviors of Family Enterprise Advisors" — 103
- Assessment Test 8 — 138

CHAPTER 9
Applying What You Have Learned — 141
Case 1 — 141
Case 2 — 142
Case 3 — 142

Glossary — 145

Suggested Readings From *Family Business Review: Journal of the Family Firm Institute* — 153

About the Website — 155

About The Family Firm Institute, Inc. — 157

About the Authors — 159

Index — 161

Acknowledgments

This book, which is the result of years of research and education undertaken by The Family Firm Institute, Inc. (FFI), would not have been possible without the intellectual collaboration and steadfast support of numerous individuals. A special debt is owed to the many members of FFI who, since 2001, have contributed to the rich body of knowledge contained herein—most especially the chairs of the Body of Knowledge Committee—Fredda Herz Brown, Karen Vinton, Mark Voeller, and Frank Hoy.

With regard to this book, we particularly want to thank co-authors Judy Green and Jane Hilburt-Davis whose leadership in the field of family enterprise advising and consulting is legendary—Judy as the president of FFI and Jane as FFI chair emeritus and curriculum developer for the FFI Global Education Network (GEN).

Thanks are also due to Paul Karofsky, who supplied the work on the cases that appear here and has provided advice and input at key stages in the development of this project.

We also want to thank John Davis, Dennis Jaffe, Cary Tutelman, and Larry Hause for permission to use their intellectual models included as part of the course.

Thanks are also due to Karen Shea of Karen Shea Design for her work on the graphics.

Family Firm Institute
Boston, Massachusetts
October 2013

Family Enterprise: Understanding Families in Business and Families of Wealth

It would not be an exaggeration to say that family enterprises are as ubiquitous as they are complex. Indeed, family enterprise is as old as humanity itself, at least in an anthropological sense. Members of families have been working together—and coming into conflict with one another—for millennia.

Of course things have changed considerably since the days when collaboration within families was simply oriented toward securing basic necessities. Today, under the imperatives of global supply chains, markets without borders, and economic interdependence, family enterprises have become powerful, and complex engines of a world economy. Many of the world's largest businesses, such as Wal-Mart, Samsung, and Tata, as well as hundreds of thousands of small to medium-sized enterprises, are family-owned and major drivers of economic output across the globe.

The purpose of this book is to clarify the complex nature and functioning of contemporary family enterprises for a wide variety of professionals—both inside and outside the family enterprise, providing an informative and cutting-edge multidisciplinary approach to the understanding of and advising to family enterprises worldwide. Although focused on the professionals in the family enterprise field, it is our hope that this information will also be useful for owners and members of family enterprises.

The book is divided into nine chapters, each of which presents essential knowledge and methods central to understanding classic approaches and current trends in the field.

The discussion begins with the challenges and opportunities peculiar to defining what, precisely, constitutes a family enterprise. While various definitions are explored and assessed, this book defines family enterprises as those with two or more members of a family involved in the ownership and business of the enterprise.

The second chapter focuses more explicitly on the classic systems of a family enterprise. Three systems, in particular, are emphasized, namely, the systems unique to the family, the ownership, and the enterprise.

The third chapter explores representative governance systems in family enterprise. Not surprisingly, family enterprises deploy a variety of governance systems that encompass family, ownership, and enterprise.

The fourth chapter highlights the key characteristics of family enterprise, including optimism, loyalty, competitiveness, innovativeness, legacy, and commitment, among others.

Chapter 5 explores relevant concepts in family enterprise study. Systems thinking and process and content, in particular, are elaborated in some detail and applied in the context of family enterprise.

Chapter 6 offers useful theoretical frameworks for analyzing and understanding family enterprises. Specifically, the three-circle model, the developmental model, and the balance point model are considered at some length.

Chapter 7 outlines the core professions most likely to engage in work with family enterprises, while Chapter 8 closes with a discussion of the importance of deploying a multidisciplinary team approach to address the challenges and opportunities facing family enterprises in today's globalized world.

Chapter 9 concludes the book with three actual cases in family enterprise. In this way the book affords readers the occasion to apply what has been learned by engaging the real world challenges and opportunities characteristically faced by those working with and within family enterprises.

Each chapter is designed to engage with relevant graphics, illustrations, and examples, as well as suggestions for further reading. Additionally, each chapter concludes with a brief self-assessment.

Taken in its entirety, this book provides a toolkit of multidisciplinary concepts, methods, examples, and assessments directly applicable to, and of use for, those engaged in the work of family enterprise. With family enterprises constituting between 65 to 80 percent of all businesses engaged in today's global economy, it is clear that providing such a toolkit is essential not only to the success of family enterprises and the professionals who work with them, but also to the future prosperity and well-being of the world's economy and the many individuals who are employed within it.

Family Enterprise

CHAPTER 1

Defining Family Enterprise

Found virtually in every sector of the world's economies, family enterprises are the most common form of business entity in the world. Yet, their ownership, management, and family composition create a complexity that requires special knowledge and skills in order to understand them and to advise them effectively.

Indeed, perhaps one of the most discussed issues in the field today is how to define a family enterprise. There is no one definition for family enterprise, but there are a few working definitions that have evolved over the years.

Family Group · Share Capital · Vision of the Business · Family Firms · Enterprise Group · Decision-making Rights · Owners · Governance · FE · FB · FIM

DEFINITION 1

Family firms are those in which multiple members of the same family are involved as major owners or managers, either contemporaneously or over time (Miller, Le-Breton Miller, Lester, Canella, "Are Family Firms Really Superior Performers," *Journal of Corporate Finance*, Vol. 13, Issue 5, 2007).

DEFINITION 2

Family firms are those in which the family controls the business through involvement in ownership and management positions. Family involvement in ownership (FIO) and family involvement in management (FIM) is measured as the percentage of equity held by family members and the percentage of a firm's managers who are also family members (Sciascia and Mazzola, *Family Business Review*, Vol. 21, Issue 4, 2008).

DEFINITION 3

A family enterprise is an economic venture (enterprise group) in which two or more members of a family (family group) have an interest in ownership (owners) and a commitment to the continuation of the enterprise.

DEFINITION 4

The family business is a business governed and/or managed with the intention to shape and/or pursue the vision of the business held by a dominant coalition controlled by members of the same family or a small number of families in a manner that is potentially sustainable across generations of the family or families.

DEFINITION 5

A firm of any size is a family business if:

1. The majority of decision-making rights are in the possession of the natural person(s) who established the firm, or in the possession of the

natural person(s) who has/have acquired the share capital of the firm, or in the possession of their spouses, parents, child, or children's direct heirs.
2. The majority of decision-making rights are indirect or direct.
3. At least one representative of the family or kin is formally involved in the governance of the firm.
4. Listed companies meet the definition of family enterprise if the person who established or acquired the firm (share capital) or their families or descendants possess 25 percent of the decision-making rights mandated by their share capital (European Union definition 2009).

The first and second definitions identified above are classic academic definitions articulated and developed by preeminent scholars in the field.

The third and fourth definitions are written by practitioners. While the first two definitions are primarily descriptive, the third and fourth are more prescriptive and place a greater emphasis on continuity.

The fifth definition is taken from the final report of the European Union's "Expert Group, Overview of Family-Business-Relevant Issues: Research, Networks, Policy Measures and Existing Studies," November 2009.

In spite of the fact that there is no one definition for family businesses, this book will define a family business in the broadest terms as one in which two or more members of a family are involved in the ownership and business of an enterprise. In fact, family, ownership, and enterprise constitute the three core systems that characteristically inform family enterprises.

KEY POINT

Family enterprises are at once the most common and the most complex form of business entity in the world today. While no single definition can be said to cover all forms of family enterprise, in the broadest sense all such enterprises have two or more members of a family involved in the ownership and business of an enterprise.

You have now finished Chapter 1. Before doing the assessments, please read the following, "From Longevity of Firms to Transgenerational Entrepreneurship of Families: Introducing Family Entrepreneurial Orientation," from *Family Business Review*.

From Longevity of Firms to Transgenerational Entrepreneurship of Families: Introducing Family Entrepreneurial Orientation

Thomas Markus Zellweger, University of St. Gallen, St. Gallen, Switzerland
Robert S. Nason, Babson College, Babson Park, MA, USA
Mattias Nordqvist, Jönköping International Business School, Jönköping, Sweden

Abstract

Whereas existing research on the longevity of family firms has focused on the survival of firms, this article investigates transgenerational entrepreneurship of families. By building on the transgenerational entrepreneurship research framework, the authors argue that by shifting from firm to family level of analysis, one gains a deeper understanding of family firms' ability to create value across generations. The authors find evidence for their argument in that such a level shift reveals extended entrepreneurial activity, which is missed when focusing exclusively on the firm level. The study introduces and empirically explores the construct of family entrepreneurial orientation, which may serve as an antecedent to transgenerational value creation by families.

Keywords

longevity, family firm, transgenerational value creation, transgenerational entrepreneurship

Introduction

John Ward's (1987) seminal study on family firm succession was the first and still remains the most influential to put a number to the rate of success in intrafamily business succession. Family business consultants and popular press journalists quote Ward's statistic that 30% of firms survive through the second generation, 13% survive the third generation, and only 3% survive beyond that. The 30/13/3 statistic has been largely unchallenged and moreover seems to suggest that there is something fundamentally "wrong" with family firms and that they inevitably fall into the three-generation survival trap. Even though these figures are often misquoted and misunderstood—for example, it has been shown that the survival rates of publicly quoted nonfamily firms are by no means larger (Aronoff, 2001)[1]—earlier family business research has contributed to this rather depressive image of family business succession. These studies often view nepotism, preservation of the status quo, and expropriation of nonfamily shareholders as main rationales for succession within the family (Fukuyama, 1995; Morck, Shleifer, & Vishny, 1988; Morck & Yeung, 2003). The literature that does focus on successful succession within family firms concentrates on building a model or identifying variables which can overcome the fundamental "problem" of succession in family firms (Le Breton-Miller, Miller, & Steier, 2004). Even in this examination of successful succession, the assumption is that there is a fundamental hurdle in all family firms which stems from family relationships complicating business activity and a CEO talent pool limited to a few family members (Le Breton-Miller et al., 2004).

Reaching beyond this gloomy picture of family succession, more recent research has shown that continued family control can be efficient, since families are, for example, able to positively affect the resource inventory and usage of their firms (Arregle, Hitt, Sirmon, & Very, 2007; Habbershon & Williams, 1999), apply a long-term perspective allowing for unique strategic positioning (Zellweger, 2007), have less agency problems and higher firm values (Anderson & Reeb, 2003), or drive new entrepreneurial activity (Kellermanns & Eddleston, 2006; Nordqvist & Melin, 2010). This research provides insights into how families make a positive contribution to their firms.

The purpose of the present study is to offer an alternative to the intrafirm succession approach to study longevity of family firms, which has dominated literature, and to explore how families become drivers of entrepreneurial activity and growth over time. More specifically, our aim is to outline a conceptual approach with the family, rather than the firm, as the relevant level of analysis for longevity and transgenerational value creation. Whereas the firm- and the individual-level perspectives have received considerable attention in entrepreneurship research (Lumpkin & Dess, 1996; Scott & Rosa, 1996), we follow calls by researchers to include family as an additional level of analysis (Astrachan, 2010; Dyer, 2003; Moores, 2009; Nordqvist & Melin, 2010; Uhlaner, Kellermanns, Eddleston, & Hoy, in press; Zahra & Sharma, 2004). Introducing such a perspective is timely because existing family firm survival studies tend to neglect the portfolio of entrepreneurial activities of business families beyond a core company and most traditional longevity studies fail to acknowledge other (appropriate) forms of succession beyond passing on the baton within the family, such as the sale of the firm as way to harvest value and create new opportunities for the family. Taken together, our article seeks to answer two main research questions: First, to what degree do business families have entrepreneurial activity beyond the core firm and dynamically adapt their portfolio of activities over time? And second, what kind of attitudes do these families exhibit toward entrepreneurial activity?

Our research seeks to make three main contributions to literature. First, we build on and refine the concept of transgenerational entrepreneurship (Habbershon, Nordqvist, & Zellweger, 2010; Habbershon & Pistrui, 2002). Second, we explore empirical evidence to justify the use of the family level of analysis in entrepreneurship research. In this pursuit, we revisit and challenge some of the assumptions and conclusions drawn in studies investigating the longevity of family firms (Le Breton-Miller et al., 2004; Ward, 1987). Third, we introduce the concept of family entrepreneurial orientation (FEO) and provide exploratory scale development. We suggest FEO to be an example of a new family-level construct, which can be developed to understand how the attitudes and mind-sets of the controlling family affect entrepreneurial activity.

Our study is structured as follows. We start with an articulation of the transgenerational entrepreneurship research framework as our theoretical lens. We continue by discussing the family as a level of analysis in entrepreneurship research and explore how such a perspective extends our understanding of longevity in family firms. Then, we present findings from an exploratory study that lends support to examining the family level of analysis. We conclude by theorizing and empirically exploring FEO and suggest several areas for future research.

Theoretical Framework: Transgenerational Entrepreneurship

To explore the processes at the family level that lead to longevity of business activity and ultimately value creation across generations, we draw on the concept of transgenerational entrepreneurship (Habbershon & Pistrui, 2002; Nordqvist & Zellweger, 2010). Habbershon et al. (2010) define transgenerational entrepreneurship as "the processes through which a family uses and develops entrepreneurial mindsets and family influenced resources and capabilities to create new streams of entrepreneurial, financial and social value across generations" (p. 1). Within this definition, the entrepreneurial mind-sets are seen as the attitudes, values, and beliefs that orient a person or a group toward the pursuit of entrepreneurial activities (Lumpkin & Dess, 1996; Miller, 1983). Entrepreneurial capabilities refer to the resources and capabilities of a given family that may facilitate entrepreneurial activities and create competitive advantage (Habbershon, Williams, & MacMillan, 2003; Sirmon & Hitt, 2003). New streams of entrepreneurial, financial, and social values refer to a broader understanding of performance and value that reaches beyond the boundaries of only economic performance outcomes in the context of families and family firms (Chrisman, Chua, & Litz, 2004; Zellweger, Nason, Nordqvist, & Brush, in press-b). Finally, the transgenerational entrepreneurship framework adopts a longitudinal perspective by looking at how value is created not only for the current stakeholders but also for the future and, in particular, future family generations. The conceptual framework, including contingency factors such as community culture, industry, family life stage, and family involvement, are depicted in Figure 1.1.[2]

Whereas the central building blocks of the model and their interconnections are laid out in Nordqvist and Zellweger (2010), the present article investigates in more detail two elements of the framework, namely (a) the level shift from firm to family

Defining Family Enterprise

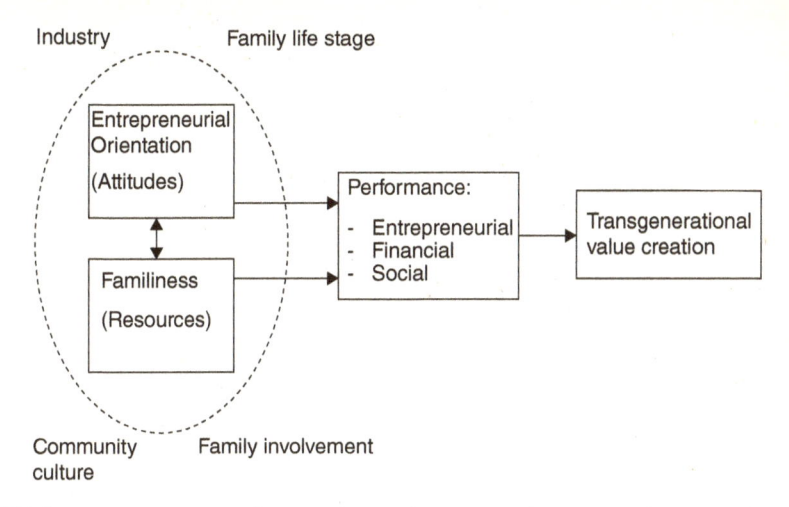

FIGURE 1.1 Transgenerational Entrepreneurship Research Framework Adapted from Nordqvist and Zellweger (2010, 9).

and its consequences for our understanding of family firm longevity and (b) the entrepreneurial mind-set of the family. The choice to focus on the entrepreneurial mind-set of the family in exploring longevity is threefold. The first is the general relevance of entrepreneurship for a firm's long-term success (Schumpeter, 1934) through renewal, innovation, and new entry (e.g., Dess et al., 2003; Zahra & Covin, 1995). Second, there is a fragmented picture regarding whether family firms represent a context encouraging or discouraging entrepreneurship (e.g., Eddleston, Kellermanns, & Zellweger, 2010; Naldi, Nordqvist, Sjöberg, & Wiklund, 2007; Schulze, Lubatkin, & Dino, 2003). Third, there is already a growing stream of literature elsewhere that focuses on family-level resources and capabilities (Danes, Stafford, Haynes, & Amarapurkar, 2009; Pearson, Carr, & Shaw, 2008; Sharma, 2008; Sieger, Zellweger, Nason, & Clinton, in press).

From the Firm to the Family Level of Analysis

A central precept of transgenerational entrepreneurship is the focus on the family itself, independent from any individual firm, just as the family's impact on entrepreneurial activity (Habbershon & Pistrui, 2002). This approach is distinct from most entrepreneurship research which focuses on either the level of the firm or the level of the individual entrepreneur (Davidsson & Wiklund, 2001). Regarding the firm level, corporate entrepreneurship studies have undertaken considerable efforts to unveil the entrepreneurial orientation of corporations (e.g., Ahuja & Lampert, 2001; Zahra, 1995). Overall, these studies have found a positive link between the level of entrepreneurial orientation in a company and its performance (Rauch, Wiklund, Lumpkin, & Frese, 2009).

In their seminal article, Low and MacMillan (1988) demonstrated that entrepreneurship is a phenomenon that occurs across levels of analysis and thus should be studied accordingly. Davidsson and Wiklund (2001) later suggested that by focusing solely on the firm level, we fail to account for sequential or parallel entrepreneurial activities undertaken by individual entrepreneurs. The rise of portfolio entrepreneurship literature has in part sought to fill this gap by shifting the level of analysis away from the firm level and toward the team or group level (Scott & Rosa, 1996; Westhead & Wright, 1998). Birley and Westhead (1994) explain the rationale behind this shift as follows:

> *If the business is the sole unit of analysis, there is a threat that the value of the new venturing event will be underestimated. It also indicates that future attempts to explain business growth should incorporate the possibility that owner-managers may attempt to resolve their personal materialistic aspirations through the growth of further business operations, which may not be directly related to the single unit of analysis being studied. (p. 57)*

Family business research exploring entrepreneurship to date has largely been conducted at the firm level. Researchers have explored firm-level phenomena such as risk taking (McConaugby, Matthews, & Fialko, 2001; Naldi et al., 2007), innovativeness (Craig & Moores, 2006), proactiveness (Daily & Dollinger, 1992), competitive aggressiveness (Zellweger & Sieger, 2010), autonomy (Donckels & Fröhlich, 1991), internationalization (Zahra, 2003), or long-term entrepreneurial strategies (Zellweger, 2007). Overall, these firm-level studies draw an inconclusive picture about the intensity and form of entrepreneurship in family firms.

Although extant literature on corporate entrepreneurship in family firms has increased our knowledge, the inconclusiveness of results is striking. Building on the transgenerational entrepreneurship framework, we contend that the uncertainty reflected in the aforementioned research is at least partly due to the neglect of the family as a distinct level of analysis. There are at least three major reasons why the family should be considered as a distinct level of analysis in future research.

First, the family represents a defining element of any family firm (Chua, Chrisman, & Sharma, 1999) and can be seen as a stakeholder category unique to this type of organization (Zellweger & Nason, 2008). The involvement of this stakeholder category imbues the firm with family elements, such as benevolent ties among actors, affect, identity concerns, and extended time-horizon on firm-level behavior (Cruz, Gomez-Mejia, & Becerra, 2010; Dyer & Whetten, 2006; Lumpkin,

Brigham, & Moss, 2010). Such firm-level outcomes of family influence include, for example, persistence with underperforming activities (Sharma & Manikutty, 2005), the inclination to take risks to preserve socioemotional wealth (Gomez-Mejia, Haynes, Nunez-Nickel, Jacobson, & Moyano-Fuentes, 2007; Zellweger, Kellermanns, Chrisman, & Chua, in press-a), and the borrowing of resources among family members to start new entrepreneurial activities (Chua, Chrisman, Kellermanns, & Wu, in press; Pearson et al., 2008; Steier, 2007). In consequence, we argue that many behavioral antecedents critical to survival and organizational success in family firms cannot be understood without inclusion of the family element (Dyer, 2003).

Second, the presence of the family as a distinct stakeholder category has an impact not only on the behavioral outcome but also on the logic guiding both the family and the firm's decision making. Families who run firms are often confronted with the management of paradoxes that emanate from the overlap of family and business systems (Nordqvist & Melin, 2010; Smith & Lewis, 2011; Tagiuri & Davis, 1996), such as balancing the wish for stability and continuity inherent in the family system and the need for adaptation and change inherent in the business system. Accordingly, and by the very nature of their constituents, family firms need to deal with competing demands to assure the persistence and the success of the combined family business system. In light of not only the resulting trade-offs but also potential synergies between family and business systems, we argue that there is a need to acknowledge the combined logic at play in the context of family firms which is neither purely family nor purely business oriented but seeks to accommodate often opposing forces.

Third, investigating the family level of analysis is further justified if the families in family firms are active in the ownership and management of multiple businesses. The implicit assumption in most longevity studies is that a family firm consists only of a single business entity. This oversimplification of the family business leads to a discourse about whether that core company either succeeds or fails in terms of remaining within family control. This perspective, however, neglects to account for family firms—even smaller ones—who start or acquire multiple firms in a portfolio of activities (Naldi, Nordqvist, & Zellweger, 2011; Sieger et al., in press). In this regard, although in an emerging stage, the research on family offices clearly demonstrates that business families are active in a diverse range of business activities (Jennings, Horan, Reichenstein, & Brunel, 2011). Although often set up on firm exit, some controlling families also set up a family office whereas still active in ownership and management of a particular firm. The family office phenomenon alone demonstrates that there is significant family-level business activity that has been almost entirely neglected with the prevailing focus on firm-level studies.

Taken together, and in line with Davidsson and Wiklund (2001), we therefore acknowledge that entrepreneurship occurs at and affects different levels and suggest that the family level has been largely neglected but warrants future attention. This is reflected in Moores's (2009) argument that family business research has reached paradigm consensus regarding (a) the focus on the business activity currently controlled by a family, (b) the neglect of the dynamic nature of entering and exiting of business activity, (c) the implicit assumption that business families control just one firm, (d) the assumption that the ideal way forward for family firms is to ensure the survival of the originally controlled firm just as close family control over this firm, and (e) the neglect of the family, as opposed to the firm or the individual entrepreneur, as the ultimate account for success and driver of economic activity. Therefore, we suggest that there is a threat to misunderstand and underestimate longevity and, more specifically, value creation through family-controlled business activity if the family as a level of analysis is not taken into consideration.

As a result of shifting the level of analysis to the family, we are not interested as much in continuity, succession, and stability of an individual family firm—which have been dominant in family business and longevity studies to date—as we are in change, growth, and the creation of the new induced by the controlling families. In short, building on Habbershon and Pistrui (2002), this level shift moves the interest from the firm to the family as the engine for entrepreneurial activities and growth across generations. Next, we show how a family-level approach addresses some of the past assumptions in previous research, creates new challenges, and provides opportunities going forward.

Consequences of Introducing the Family Level of Analysis

From family business to business family portfolio. The primary consequence of shifting the level of analysis to the family is related to the scope of business activity under examination. Recent studies show that even small to midsized family firms often engage in corporate strategy (Naldi et al., 2011). As such, by solely focusing on the most visible and often oldest firm controlled by a family, we fail to account for other business activities undertaken by the family. Business families may add new ventures, business units, or firms, for example under a holding structure, extending ownership to a group of individuals rather than one individual, with or without nonfamily participation. In this vein, Carter and Ram (2003) argue that "an analysis of the wider literature suggests that for many small firms, family circumstances may influence both the decision to engage in portfolio strategies and also the processes which are used in the portfolio approach." A growing literature around family-controlled portfolio entrepreneurship also challenges this core company view (Carter & Ram, 2003; Plate, Schiede, & von Schlippe, 2010; Scott & Rosa, 1996; Sieger et al., in press; Westhead & Wright, 1998).

Definition of family business. Shifting the level of analysis to the family and exploring a broader range of business activities challenges us to revisit the very definition of family business both structurally and temporally. It is essential to consider the many changes in ownership, board, and management structure occurring in all firms over time, which can affect whether a firm is deemed "family" or "nonfamily." For example, the transition from a sole family owner-manager, to a nonfamily CEO with continued family ownership may mean that this firm loses its "family business" status under the strictest definitions and would have to be qualified as a failure in the traditional succession and longevity logic (Chua et al., 1999; Ward, 1987).

We can also reexamine the temporal dimension in the definition of a family business proposed by Chua et al. (1999) with a transgenerational entrepreneurship mind-set. They note

> *The family business is a business governed and/or managed with the intention to shape and pursue the vision of the business held by a dominant coalition controlled by members of the same family or a small number of families in a manner that is potentially sustainable across generations of the family or families. (Chua et al., 1999, p. 25)*

If a family is holding multiple businesses, the family may not intend to control or continue to shape the strategy of any individual business across generations, but rather to control and to shape the strategy of a collection of firms and business activities across a limited holding period.

For this reason, when studying longevity through the lens of transgenerational entrepreneurship, it is important to use a family business definition which is broad enough to encompass family-controlled entrepreneurial activity despite alterations in governance and activity type across time.

Success and failure in family firms. Related to the definitional questions, introducing the family as the level of analysis requires that we reexamine how success and failure are characterized in family firms. Following the definition of a family firm as a single entity which is intended to remain under family control, business exit is always seen as a failure. In John Ward's (1987) original sample of 200 manufacturing firms in Illinois, it is true that only 13% remained intact and under family control through the third generation. However, it was actually 20% of the firms which survived. Of the remaining 7%, 5% were sold to outsiders and 2% went public. Applying a transgenerational entrepreneurship perspective, this

7% would not be seen as a failure but rather likely a success for two reasons. First, the family may retain control of a firm that goes public through voting rights or other control mechanisms (Faccio & Lang, 2002); in fact, we know that 35% of publically traded *Fortune* 500 companies remain family controlled (Anderson & Reeb, 2003). Second, and more important, the strategic move to exit a business may further greatly increase family wealth and resources to be redeployed in other business opportunities (DeTienne, 2010; Mason & Harrison, 2006).

Under the transgenerational entrepreneurship frame, a different perspective of failure is needed if a firm under family control is closed down. The transgenerational entrepreneurship approach follows Sharma and Manikutty (2005) who contend,

for firms desirous of longevity as family firms of interest to us, changes in the environment require strategic responses on the part of a firm (such as readjustment of the business portfolio and divestment of unproductive resources), so as to enable regeneration and renewal. (p. 295)

This means that the divestment or closure of a business may actually be the opposite of failure, but necessary to sustain a competitive advantage and ensure longevity for family-controlled business activity eventually in a new setting. In fact, recent research indicates that previous entrepreneurial failures can have a positive impact on growth of future entrepreneurial ventures (Yamakawa, Peng, & Deeds, 2010).

The family as a unitary actor. Although shifting to the family level of analysis seems appropriate, it also raises unique challenges. When trying to explore a family level of analysis, it seems fair to challenge the *unity* of families, and thus the appropriateness of family as a *unit* of analysis (Nordqvist & Melin, 2010). Like firms and organizations, business families are constituted by several individuals who may not always agree on all issues while working together. Families, like organizations, are dynamic as they evolve and change over time—members come and go. Examples of tensions, disagreements, and conflicts are often very destructive and span several generations and branches of families and are indeed manifold, not the least in family business literature (cf. Gordon & Nicholson, 2008; Levinson, 1971).

At the same time, however, many families have an astounding ability to align their views and act united in situations where it is mostly needed. In fact, a key feature of the family is its tendency to perpetuate its existence by ensuring its integration, despite threats of dilapidation and dispersion (Bourdieu, 1996). Sociologists and economists have long considered the family a central actor in both the social and economic realms. For example, Berger and Luckmann (1966) suggest that the family is one of the strongest and most unified societal institutions. Family is seen as one of the "key sites of the accumulation of capital in its different forms and its transmission between the generations. It safeguards its unity for and through this transmission" (Bourdieu, 1996, p. 23). Bourdieu (1996) contends that the family acts as a collective subject in such activities even more than internally weaker institutions such as firms do. Such a perspective of treating a family as a unitary actor is in line with a common practice among social scientists to attribute properties and opinions of an individual to that of a group (Nordqvist & Melin, 2010).

Supporting such a unitary actor view, Nordqvist and Melin (2010) argue that even if a family refers to a collective of individuals, there is often, like in organizations and firms, a dominant actor or a coalition of actors that represents a vision above others which determines the future of the family's entrepreneurial activities (Chua et al., 1999; Cyert & March, 1963).

Taken together, despite possible differences among family members, and just as is done for firm-level studies, there are good arguments to treat a family as a unitary actor and a collective subject given the unifying forces at play, such as social norms for harmony and mutual support not to mention the factual inability to leave one's family.

Families as basal system of economic activity and the accrual of wealth. Whereas management scholars see the firm as the engine and the account for growth, the level shift of analysis implies that we assign the same role to families. In consequence, the ultimate measure and account for success is the degree to which a family is able to generate value and ultimately wealth. Accordingly, it seems inappropriate or at least insufficient to use firm-level outcomes such as survival, independence, size, or performance of single organizations as the sole account of success for a family's wealth creation abilities.

Exploratory Findings of Entrepreneurial Activity at the Family Level

At this early stage of theorizing that families are the drivers of entrepreneurial activity, it seems premature to suggest causal relationships between family attributes and the level and form of entrepreneurial activity controlled by families. Accordingly, we refrain from developing hypotheses on such relationships. Rather, and in an exploratory manner, we collected data on the broad relevance of our phenomenon of interest, which is the level of entrepreneurial activity undertaken by families. In this regard, we hope to offer an introductory test to see if further research focusing on the family rather than the firm level is justified. More specifically, we collected data about the degree to which a business family is involved beyond a core company and the evolution of the family's entrepreneurial activities over the family's history. Through these questions we attempt to capture both the breadth and historic development of a family's entrepreneurial activity.

Method

To answer these questions we crafted an electronic survey that was sent to respondents from two address data sets: the first data set stems from the Family Firm Institute, Boston, which sent the link to the survey to their members ($n = 1,600$) asking them to forward the link to their family business contacts. One reminder e-mail was sent out to increase the response rate. The second data set stems from Babson College that sent the survey to students and alumni who attended family business classes during the past 4 years ($n = 921$). Again, one reminder e-mail was used to increase response rate. In total, we received answers from 541 respondents—all family members and owners—resulting in an aggregate response rate of 21%. We then screened the responses for quality purposes and only included data sets in our analysis where respondents had provided answers to all questions. Whereby this measure increased the quality of our data, it also significantly reduced the number of respondents to 118 data sets (5% response rate). Although this response rate is lower than expected it is not uncommon in surveys sent to family business owners and managers. The reason for the large number of incomplete questionnaires may be threefold. First, members of Family Firm Institute (most of them consultants and other service providers) might have taken a look at the survey to judge whether they wanted to forward the survey to their clients, and thereby created an entry with incomplete data in our database. Second, we included a branching question at the beginning of the survey asking whether there is a controlling family holding at least 50% of the voting rights of at least one company with at least at second-generation family involvement in the businesses. Although this question assured data gathering about family firms with a transgenerational perspective, it meant that respondents started filling out the survey thereby leaving an entry in the database but dropped out if they did not meet the aforementioned criteria. Third, the number of incomplete surveys may be particularly high due to the confidentiality of certain questions, such as total sales volumes of all firms controlled by the family, and because of the difficulty to answer certain questions, such as the number of businesses controlled over a family's continued business activity. This drop in number of responses is significant, however not uncommon and needs to be balanced against the increase in data quality and reliability of our findings.

To investigate the degree to which a business family is involved beyond a core company, we collected data on the number of firms currently controlled by the family and the sales volume of the individual firms being part of the family's extended portfolio of business activity. To answer how the family's entrepreneurial activities evolved over the family's history, we collected data on the number of firms controlled over family history, the number of firms added through mergers and acquisitions, number of firms divested over family history, and the number of industry shifts. To complete the picture, we also collected data on ownership control by the family in the individual firms and the involvement of the family in operations (number of family and nonfamily employees).

Results for Entrepreneurial Activity at the Family Level

Overall, 75.4% of our respondents indicate that their firms' headquarters are located in Northern America, 8.5% in Latin America, 7.6% in Europe, 6.8% in Africa and 1.7% in Asia. Even though our sample has an international focus, our findings are, thus particularly, reflecting the North American context. The mean age of family control in the family's core company is 60.2 years,[3] with the 2.8th family generation being in control. On average, the sales volume of the total business activity by the extended family amounts to US$173.7 million. The mean number of full-time nonfamily employees in these activities is 491 and 3.9 family employees. The mean ownership stake of the family amounts to 93.4%.

Table 1.1 reports the current and past entrepreneurial activity of the controlling families who responded to our survey.

Table 1.1 provides exploratory yet striking evidence of entrepreneurial activity beyond a core firm. In fact, only 10.6% of our respondents indicate that they control just a single firm. The mean number of firms currently controlled by the family is 3.4 firms, whereby the core company on average makes up roughly three quarter of total sales of the family-controlled business activity, that is, the family business group.

Also, Table 1.1 provides testimony of strong entrepreneurial activity across time. On average and over the family's history these families controlled 6.1 firms, created 5.4 firms, added 2.7 firms through merger and acquisition activity, spun off 1.5 firms, and shifted industry focus 2.1 times. Put differently, these families exhibit a significant level of entrepreneurial activity over time, in terms of rearrangements of the portfolio of activities through founding activity, mergers and acquisitions, as well as divestments. If indeed families serve as drivers of entrepreneurial activity, the second research question explored is, what then is the family-level mind-set that leads to entrepreneurial activities?

Toward Family Entrepreneurial Orientation

This preliminary evidence of entrepreneurial activity beyond a core business seems to suggest that further study of business activity on the family level is justified. In the following section, we theorize and provide preliminary empirical testing for a construct that taps into the family-level mind-set to engage in entrepreneurial activity. We call this concept family entrepreneurial orientation (FEO) and define it as the attitudes and mind-sets of families to engage in entrepreneurial activity.

TABLE 1.1 Entrepreneurial Activity of Controlling Family

Descriptive statistics	Mean	SD
Years of continuous family control of core company	60.2	44
Number of employees across all companies controlled by family		
Nonfamily employees	491	1,724
Family employees	3.9	3.0
Ownership stake of the family in core company	93.4	14.5
Largest firm (sales)	US$3.02 billion	
Oldest firm	384 years	
Current entrepreneurial activity of the family beyond core company		
Total sales volume of family business group, whereof	US$174 million	US$362 million
74% Core company		
18% Second company		
8% Third company and beyond		
No. of companies currently controlled by family	3.4	3.3
Share of respondents: Family controls one company	10.6%	
Share of respondents: Family controls two companies	44.7%	
Share of respondents: Family controls three companies	12.8%	
Share of respondents: Family controls four companies	10.6%	
Share of respondents: Family controls five or more companies	21.3%	
Entrepreneurial activity over the family's history	**Mean**	**SD**
No. of companies controlled over family history	6.1	12.3
No. of companies founded over family history	5.4	10.9

Entrepreneurial activity over the family's history	Mean	SD
No. of companies added through merger and acquisition over family history	2.7	4.7
No. of companies spun off over family history	1.5	3.3
Times main industry shifted over history of business activity	2.1	1.2

Note. Definitions: *Core company*—the largest firm within the family business group in terms of sales volume. There are family business groups that only consist of one company, which is then defined as the core company. *Family business group*—the entirety of the business portfolio controlled by the business family. The family business group can consist of one or multiple companies.

Martin and Lumpkin (2003) introduce the notion of family orientation and contrast it with entrepreneurial orientation at the firm level. They suggest that an increasing family orientation will overtake the entrepreneurial orientation as the family firm is passed on through generations. Their family orientation dimensions are interdependency, loyalty, security, stability, and tradition (Martin & Lumpkin, 2003). These authors thus argue for a trade-off view between entrepreneurial and family orientation where both postures cannot exist simultaneously. According to this incongruence perspective it should therefore be unlikely that family firms will survive over long periods of time, given the necessity for firms to adapt to an ever-changing environment and hence be entrepreneurial to a certain degree. In their view, sooner or later, family firms should fall prey to inertia and will go out of business due to family orientation suffocating entrepreneurial orientation. However, the empirical reality challenges this assumption—family firms that are generations and even centuries old exist in great numbers. For example, in our sample (notably dominated by North American firms), 12.7% of all firms were more than 100 years old.

At the same time, it seems inappropriate to simply extend traditional corporate entrepreneurship measures to the family level. Such an approach intending to find aspects that entrepreneurship and family business share is limited in terms of its explicative power. If the goal is to study family businesses through the lens of entrepreneurship, the appropriate approach will have to define what actually is relevant to study given the characteristics of the family firm context. In other words, since the individual and organizational aspects represented in dominant corporate entrepreneurship approaches do not cover specific family-related factors, it is unsatisfactory to just apply these approaches to explain transgenerational entrepreneurship without appropriate contextualization.

Indeed, scholars have aired important concerns about the applicability of traditional entrepreneurship constructs such as entrepreneurial orientation to the context of family firms. For example, Nordqvist, Habbershon, and Melin (2008), Zellweger and Sieger (2010), and Lumpkin et al. (2010) all suggest that whereas risk-taking and competitive aggressiveness are less important to family firms, autonomy, innovativeness, and proactiveness are more important and have greater meaning for transgenerational value creation. These authors also suggest a distinction between internal and external autonomy (independence of business units and teams within a firm vs. independence from external stakeholders) as well as internal and external innovativeness (internal innovativeness defined as the innovation in terms of processes and structures within the firm, vs. external innovativeness, defined as new products or new market entry). To an established scale, these distinctions and refinements question its overall applicability for the specific family firm context.

Martin and Lumpkin (2003) are helpful in that they point at the relevance of dimensions such as interdependency, loyalty, security, stability, and tradition, which simultaneously coexist with the need for change, innovation, risk-taking, and growth. A possible measure of FEO therefore needs to combine attributes that are prototypical of the family *and* business domains. In consequence, a FEO scale should, on one hand, incorporate attitudes such as security, control, stability, and tradition. These attributes are reflective of a family's goal to assure the family's oneness and the family's wish for control over the activities undertaken across time (Albert & Whetten, 1985; Bourdieu, 1996; Nordqvist & Melin, 2010; Zellweger et al., in press-a). On the other hand, and to cover firm-related attitudes toward entrepreneurial behavior, FEO should include items covering autonomy within the firm, innovation orientation, proactiveness, and the willingness to take risk.

The notion of FEO thus seeks to capture bivalent attributes and the resulting tensions in family firms (Tagiuri & Davis, 1996). Such a perspective alludes to Nordqvist et al. (2008), who draw on the five dimensions of entrepreneurial orientation and integrate the concept of duality to interpret what characterizes entrepreneurship in family firms over time. They identify three dualities related to the dimensions of entrepreneurial orientation: the historical/new path duality, the independence/dependence duality, and the formality/informality duality. Nordqvist et al. (2008) thus implicitly suggest that instead of maximizing their entrepreneurial orientation at any point in time, long-term value-creating family firms seem to manage these dualities to combine the attributes of family and business. Such an argument for the quest of an equilibrium between stability and change is largely supported by Zellweger and Sieger (2010) who suggest that entrepreneurial orientation is applied or misunderstood as a normative concept of the "right" entrepreneurial behavior and that more entrepreneurial orientation is always better. These concerns are related to the observation that many newly established firms are highly entrepreneurial but unable to survive more than a few years (Audretsch, 1991).

Early family business scholars and scholars rooted in economics have taken an approach to these tensions by claiming that the business system is superior to the family system in creating value across time and hence the business logic should dominate the family logic (*trade-off perspective*; e.g., Levinson, 1971; Morck & Yeung, 2003). More recently, scholars have started taking a *contingency perspective* by exploring the conditions under which family is beneficial or detrimental to a firm. The idea here is to separate the extremes structurally, temporarily, and spatially, seeking for the situations under which the tensions were most effective. Scholars of this tradition have, for example, explored the alignment of different resource configurations and the quality of interactions (Eddleston & Kellermanns, 2007; Eddleston, Kellermanns, & Sarathy, 2008), and the quality of the institutional setting (Gedajlovic, Carney, Chrisman, & Kellermanns, 2011).

In contrast to contingency theory, a *paradox perspective*, which we suggest for the FEO concept, assumes that tensions persist within complex and dynamic systems such as in family firms. Similar to the duality approach mentioned above, such a paradox perspective can shift the attention asked by contingency theorists from identifying the conditions under which organizations are more driven by certain factors (e.g., stability vs. change orientation or family vs. business interests) to how firms engage in these competing factors simultaneously (Smith & Lewis, 2011). Such a paradox perspective moves away from the original meaning of paradox, which is simultaneous existence of at least two incompatible dimensions. Previous family business research has shown that family and business factors are not necessarily incompatible but can indeed be synergistic (Basco & Perez-Rodriguez, 2009; Stewart & Hitt, 2010; Zellweger & Nason, 2008). Focusing on the underlying tensions as dualities between two elements, the definition of paradox suggested by Smith and Lewis (2011) is useful for our purpose. They view paradox as "contradictory yet interrelated elements that exist simultaneously and persist over time" (Smith & Lewis, 2011, p. 382). This definition highlights two components of paradox: (a) underlying tensions, that is, elements that seem logical individually but inconsistent and even absurd when juxtaposed and (b) responses that embrace tensions simultaneously (Lewis, 2000).

In this context, managers are urged to overcome disjunctions, to seek synergies between the two, and to strive to harness efficiency advantages from the complexity. This perspective is in line with an emergent "systemic" view (Luhmann, 1984) that has been tentatively addressed in recent family business research (Basco & Perez-Rodriguez, 2009; Frank, Lueger, Nose, & Suchy, 2010; Habbershon et al., 2003; Litz, 2008; Schuman, Stutz, & Ward, 2010; Simon, 2006; Stewart & Hitt, 2010; Zellweger & Nason, 2008).

Results for Exploratory Scale Building for Family Entrepreneurial Orientation

It is beyond the purpose of this study to develop and test a full-fledged scale of FEO. Instead, we have conducted an exploratory empirical survey with the aim of making first steps toward a future establishment of such a scale. In these attempts, we have followed guidance from the scale-building literature (Churchill, 1979; Hinkin, 1995; Liu, Chua, & Stahl, 2010).

In a first step, and building on above considerations about the appropriate content of an FEO scale, defined as the attitudes and mind-sets of families to engage in entrepreneurial activity, we selected items that had a priori content validity given our concern for family and business-related dimensions, as outlined above. On the side of the family we incorporated attitudes such as security, control, stability, and transgenerational orientation (Lumpkin, Martin, & Vaughn, 2008). Regarding firm-related attitudes toward entrepreneurial behavior we included autonomy, innovativeness, proactiveness, and risk-taking, following guidance in the corporate entrepreneurship literature, as outlined above (Covin & Slevin, 1991; Lumpkin & Dess, 1996; Zahra, 2005). We also considered the distinctiveness of internal and external types of autonomy (Nordqvist et al., 2008; Zellweger & Sieger, 2010). In addition, we included items related to resource focus and the formality of strategizing. The reason was to be able to forge links between the traditional EO measures and resource management, which has received increased attention in family business literature (Chrisman, Chua, & Sharma, 2005; Sirmon & Hitt, 2003) and transgenerational entrepreneurship writings (Nordqvist & Zellweger, 2010).

In a next step, we discussed the concept and items with senior scholars in the field[4] and shortened the scale. Following scale-building literature (Churchill, 1979), we then conducted a pretest with two U.S.-based families and incorporated feedback to clarify items. The resulting items and the introductory question are provided in Table 1.2.

These items were included in the survey outlined above. Given the sample size of 118 respondents our analysis exhibits an item to response ratio of 10.1 (=118 respondents/11 items) which is well above the threshold of 4 (Hinkin, 1995). We then conducted an exploratory factor analysis with varimax rotation to extract a number of uncorrelated components describing FEO, which resulted in four components with eigenvalues greater than 1. Together these four factors account for 63.8% of the variance.

We then investigated the meaningfulness and postrotation loadings of the components. Although the first two components seemed meaningful and exhibited postrotation loadings >2, Components 3 and 4 were not retained.

TABLE 1.2 Items for Family Entrepreneurial Orientation and Results of Exploratory Factor Analysis

		\multicolumn{4}{c}{Component (varimax rotation)}			
Item description	Introductory question: "The family as a whole . . ."	1	2	3	4
Preservation orientation	. . . strives to preserve existing businesses/strives to create new businesses.	**.804**	.174	−.012	.206
Transgenerational outlook	. . . makes decisions primarily with the success of the current generation in mind/makes decisions primarily with the success of future generations in mind.	**.730**	.115	−.093	−.023
Change orientation	. . . is resistant to change/is very willing to change.	**.655**	.333	−.317	−.069
Autonomy (external)	. . . is highly dependent on relationships with external stakeholders to grow the business/is not at all dependent on external stakeholders to grow the business.	**.505**	−.089	.381	−.421
Risk orientation	. . . favors low-risk projects with normal and certain rates of return/favors high-risk projects with chances of very high returns.	.074	**.849**	−.085	−.136
Resource focus	. . . pursues opportunities with close attention to the resources we currently control/pursues opportunities without regard to resources currently controlled.	.145	**.676**	.328	.162
Proactiveness	. . . is seldom the first to introduce new products/	.216	**.628**	−.076	.084

(*Continued*)

TABLE 1.2 (*Continued*)

	Component (varimax rotation)				
Item description	Introductory question: "The family as a whole . . ."	1	2	3	4
	services, technologies, and so on/is often the first to introduce new products/services, technologies, and so on.				
Innovativeness	. . . favors a strong emphasis on existing internal processes (e.g., managerial, technological)/favors a strong emphasis on new internal processes (e.g., managerial, technological).	.544	**.552**	–.103	.069
Stability versus growth	. . . values growth and expansion/values stability and continuity.	–.172	–.321	**.766**	.075
Formality of strategizing	. . . tends to grow through a formal strategy/rends to grow through an informal strategy.	–.083	.254	**.672**	.040
Autonomy (internal)	. . . allows individuals/teams to pursue business opportunities on their own/expects individuals/teams pursuing business opportunities to obtain approval from their supervisor(s).	.102	.026	.127	**.892**

Note. Items loading on the same component in bold.

Components 3 and 4 consist of two, respectively, one item and exhibit relatively weak postrotation loadings of 1.44 and 1.08. Moreover, we had concerns about content validity. Cronbach's alpha for Component 1 was .613 but could be improved to .728 in case the external stakeholder dependence item (external autonomy) was deleted. The same assessment for Component 2 resulted in a satisfactory alpha of .736. No improvements in alpha could be achieved by omitting one of the items. Since Component 1 covers aspects such as value generation for future generations and willingness to change and create new businesses, we decided to label this item *transgenerational entrepreneurial orientation* of the family. Component 2, in contrast, captures *risk and innovation orientation* of the family. Taken together, although our survey development efforts for measurement of FEO resulted in a two-factor, eight-item measure, the reliability measures indicate that further item development is needed to refine the scale before it can be used in substantive theory testing.

Discussion

Whereas the firm and the individual entrepreneur levels have received considerable attention in strategy, entrepreneurship, and family business research (Lumpkin & Dess, 1996; Scott & Rosa, 1996), we follow calls by researchers to include family as an additional level of analysis when investigating family firms and their longevity (Dyer, 2003; Moores, 2009; Nordqvist & Melin, 2010; Zahra & Sharma, 2004). The inclusion of the family as a distinct level of analysis is warranted because the family stakeholder category with its particular logic has a crucial impact on firm-level behaviors (Gomez-Mejia et al., 2007) and because business families often control more than a single firm (Naldi et al., 2011; Naldi et al., Sieger et al., in press). Therefore, to unveil the scope and longevity of family-controlled business activity it is misleading to just focus on a single organizational entity.

Moving from the family business to the entirety of family-related business activity and assessing its evolution in a longitudinal manner has important consequences for our understanding of family firms and their longevity. It is essential to consider the many changes in ownership, board, and management structure occurring in firms over time, which can affect whether a firm is deemed "family" or "nonfamily." When studying longevity through the transgenerational entrepreneurship perspective, we cannot accept a narrow definition of family firms or organizational failure as divestments, as even firm failure can be useful for long-term value creation (Yamakawa et al., 2010). Just as importantly, when a next-generation family member is unwilling to take over from parents, this may not be seen as failure but as a value-creating strategy in light of other options for the firm and its leadership. Also, the level shift from firm to family further implies a focus on the portfolio of business activities of the family, beyond the single firm, and sees the family as the appropriate vehicle to assess whether value and wealth are created or destroyed over time. Finally, shifting from the family to the firm implies a unitary perspective of the family, despite potential intrafamily differences in preferences and perspectives.

Our preliminary empirical investigation of entrepreneurial activity at the family level provides exploratory data on the importance of such a level shift. Roughly 90% of the families responding to our survey indicate that they control more than a single firm. Our results suggest that there is strong entrepreneurial activity undertaken by controlling families beyond their core (i.e., largest) company. It is important to note here that in the traditional succession and longevity logic, families in our sample would be accountable for 2.7 failed firms over time (6.1 firms controlled over history—3.4 firms currently controlled). In the transgenerational entrepreneurship logic, however, these rearrangements of the business portfolio, in particular the firms divested or closed, may be seen as value-enhancing activities that advance the wealth position of the family as a whole.

Beyond the shift in level of analysis our study explores a further building block of transgenerational entrepreneurship, namely FEO, defined as the attitudes and mind-sets of families to engage in entrepreneurial activity. We argue that this family-level scale needs to combine attributes that are prototypical of the family domain—such as interdependency, stability, and transgenerational outlook—with attributes that are exemplary of the business domain—such as change, innovation, and risk orientation. The notion of FEO thus seeks to capture these bivalent attributes and the resulting tensions in family firms (Tagiuri & Davis, 1996). In such a paradox perspective the family and business logic seem logical individually but inconsistent and or even absurd when juxtaposed (Lewis, 2000). The argument of seeing FEO as a mix of family and business logic follows the systemic tradition according to which organizations have to attend to competing and often paradoxical demands simultaneously (Smith & Lewis, 2011). Both systems, family and business, are definitional and hence integral part of the family firm reality. They persist over time and cannot be separated from each other. Accordingly, the various tensions within family firms (for instance between stability and change, innovation and tradition, short-term and long-term orientation, family first and business first) cannot be resolved by the annihilation of the respective other dimension (Stewart & Hitt, 2010) and should therefore both be captured in an FEO scale.

With our, admittedly tentative, scale-building attempt, we have sketched out a possible FEO scale and identified two underlying components that are reflective of our considerations about combining family and business orientation in a combined measure: *transgenerational entrepreneurial orientation* and *risk and innovation orientation*. The first component, transgenerational entrepreneurial orientation, is particularly worth discussing in more depth. This dimension includes elements typically assigned to the business sphere such as creating new firms and at the same time also includes the family element of decision making with the next-generation mind. The fact that these seemingly opposing statements load on the same component reflect the synergistic perspective outlined above. Families are willing to foster change and growth of business activities, but they do so for the benefit of the next generation, and not solely the immediate benefit of the current owners. In addition, although previous literature has been divided with regard to how important innovation and risk-taking are for entrepreneurial development and longevity of family firms (Naldi et al., 2007; Schulze et al., 2003; Zahra, 2005), our preliminary findings suggest that risk and innovation are critical components of a business family's entrepreneurial orientation.

Seeing family and business perspectives as nonsubstitutable alludes to recent ambidexterity literature which suggests that organizations need to be aligned to both exploitation and exploration (Andriopoulos & Lewis, 2009; He & Wong, 2004; March, 1991; Sharma & Salvato, in press). Just as a one-sided exploitation may enhance short-term performance but can result in a complacency and competency trap because firms may not be able to respond adequately to environmental changes (Gibson & Birkinshaw, 2004), a one-sided focus on family can result in similar constraints. Conversely, just as too much exploration admittedly enhances a firm's ability to renew its knowledge base, it may spark endless cycles of trial and error. In analogy to this perspective, an excessive emphasis of business over family logic may undermine trust-based family relationships, reduce family commitment and, for instance, willingness to lend patient capital and can limit the value creation potential through the synergies from family involvement. Just as March's (1991) argument that successful firms are ambidextrous, contributed to a general shift in organizational research from trade-off to paradoxical thinking (Eisenhardt, 2000; Gavetti & Levinthal, 2000; Lewis, 2000), when trying to investigate longevity of family firms we suggest a shift to paradox thinking as reflected in our FEO concept. Taken together, just as firms are ambidextrous when able to simultaneously accommodate exploration and exploitation tendencies, our understanding of FEO suggests business families to be ambidextrous and ultimately value creating across generations if they are able to simultaneously accommodate paradoxical family and business orientations.

Limitations and Future Research

We need to point to some limitations of our study, most of which are related to the exploratory nature of the empirical part of our research. In addition to the limited sample size, our study may be affected by selection bias. In fact, the introductory question to our survey asking for family majority voting control in at least one company may have led to an overrepresentation of firms with multiple businesses in their portfolio, thereby inflating the evidence of portfolio activity. Given the address data sets we used, midsized to large firms are likely to be overrepresented. Accordingly, our findings may be particularly applicable to this type of firm.

Asking for business activity over time requires a level of familiarity with the evolution of entrepreneurial activity of the family, whereby older respondents may be more knowledgeable. However, in light of the mean age of our respondents of 49.2 years we have no indication that especially elder people should have filled out the survey, and hence would have inflated the level of family-controlled business activity over time. Our study may be affected by differing definitions of the family. How extended is the family? Who is part of it, and accordingly, what business activity is part of the family's portfolio of activities? While the various definitions of family represent a challenge, especially in cross-national studies of entrepreneurship because of the differing meaning of family across cultures, the impact of this aspect is likely to be limited in the present study given that the majority of firms in our sample are from North America. On the downside, we are not able to extend our findings to cultures and nations outside North America.

Also, our scale-building attempts are exploratory at best. Scale-building literature suggests that two data sets should be used to validate scales (Churchill, 1979). Unfortunately, however, we just have one sample at hand, and it is too small for a sample split. In addition, we did not perform a confirmatory factor analysis to further validate the distinctiveness of the two components of FEO. Given these restrictions we refrained from developing hypotheses about relationships between these components and some outcome variable.

Moreover, our data are affected by survivor bias. Part of the influence of John Ward's original study was his meticulous methodology to track individual firms over their history and note when firms "died." Given the resource constraints to this research, large-scale duplication of John Ward's methodology was not possible. Since we are only able to study living cases and not able to track firms that have disappeared or have reemerged, our findings are biased by the fact that we are investigating firms that have been successful in many of the dimensions we are investigating. Furthermore, we do not explore philanthropic activities, family offices, or to what extent families loan money to relatives to start their own businesses. These are all important areas for future research.

Future research can be designed to address these limitations. In fact, our study opens up a wide set of research opportunities. First of all, we suggest replicating our exploratory empirical study on a random sample of business families. More specifically, strategy and family business scholars have only started to look into the corporate strategy making and portfolio activities of business families. For too long, family firms have been assumed to be run as a single business entity by an owner-manager. As our research indicates, business families are often engaged in several businesses as a way to grow their total economic activity. More research is needed to better understand the drivers and motives behind this entrepreneurial behavior of families (Sieger et al., in press). Future research can also investigate how heirs use either inheritance money or trust fund money to fund their own business ventures. This may be a particularly common practice as businesses get older and branches on the family tree multiply; it then becomes an important way for family businesses to create transgenerational value.

Further attempts are needed to advance toward a scale of FEO. The challenge related to building such a scale is that it simultaneously combines family and business elements. The items and components in Table 1.2 may just be starting points in this direction. More solid scale-building attempts are needed to advance in such a direction. In doing so, the various scale-building methodologies will be helpful (Churchill, 1979; Hinkin, 1995; Liu et al., 2010; Schwab, 1980).

Alternatively, researchers could adhere to the empirical methodologies within ambidexterity literature. One way of advancing along this path is to investigate how various degrees of family orientation—measured through Lumpkin et al.'s (2008) family orientation dimensions, for example—combined with various degrees of business orientation—measured, for instance, through growth expectancies of the controlled activities—affect the transgenerational value creation in the controlled firm(s). Researchers could investigate how a family that scores high on both logics affects value creation, in which case the product (Family orientation * Business orientation) would be a good proxy for ambidexterity. Alternatively, a family may be regarded as ambidextrous if it displays relatively equal emphasis on both logics. In this balanced approach, one would have to take the difference (family orientation – business orientation) as the proxy for family ambidexterity. In this case, even a firm that puts low emphasis on both dimensions would be classified as ambidextrous (Andriopoulos & Lewis, 2009; He & Wong, 2004; Raisch & Birkinshaw, 2008).

Finally, as FEO is a construct intended to be measured on the family level of analysis, we believe that it may also be useful in helping explain a new set of family-level dependent variables in future research. Future research may attempt to measure total wealth accumulated by families across generations or entrepreneurial activity across generations. Exploring these dependent variables for future research would be most appreciated since it could give voice to our more fundamental observation that families and not only entrepreneurs or individual firms are drivers of economic growth and prosperity.

Implications for Practice

Our proposed approach to longevity in family firms has several important implications for practice. By shifting the level of analysis to the family, business families can decouple family and firm life stage in a way that may lead to the creation of new streams of value over time. Seeing a family's entrepreneurial orientation as a critical antecedent to transgenerational value creation, it may be important to shift a family's self-understanding from controlling a "family business" to being an "entrepreneurial family."

Second, this article offers an alternative approach to the often contentious process of succession in family firms. For those firms that view the family as the wealth creation vehicle and strive to create new businesses over time, they may be able to move beyond the succession model which is based on identifying the single most competent heir to become the CEO. Rather, when there are multiple firms or the opportunity to create new firms, there are also multiple leadership roles for next-generation family members. Next-generation family members may not only take over the core family firm, but they may also start a new firm, create value by developing a philanthropic arm, and lead a major new initiative within the family firm—for instance franchising or taking a manufacturing company into retail.

Third, those who wish to intentionally integrate entrepreneurial behavior into their business family need to find mechanisms and structures which facilitate this in a way that is not tied to a single firm. Although further work needs to be done to study their effectiveness, a few examples include creating an internal family venture fund, a family-controlled holding company, an incubator for new ventures, or an online family forum for sharing ideas.

Conclusion

We believe that our study contributes to the ongoing and important debate about longevity in family firms by redirecting the discussion to the family level of analysis. Such a family-centered perspective that takes into account the total entrepreneurial activity of a family has been conspicuously overlooked in the literature to date and significantly adds to our understanding of family firm longevity and transgenerational value creation of families. Our exploratory study offers initial insights into how we might reframe the longevity and succession discussion in family firms and stimulate promising research about transgenerational entrepreneurship and value creation.

Acknowledgments

We wish to thank Joe Goodman for his financial support of this research and the Family Firm Institute for its award and support, and in particular its Executive

Director, Dr. Judy Green, for her encouragement during the research process. We would also like to thank Dr. Allison Pearson, our editor at *Family Business Review*, for her insightful guidance throughout the review process, as well as the two anonymous reviewers.

Authors' Note

This article uses data collected as part of the Family Firm Institute–Goodman Longevity Study.

Declaration of Conflicting Interests

The author(s) declared no potential conflicts of interest with respect to the research, authorship, and/or publication of this article.

Funding

The author(s) received financial support through the Joe Goodman Award from the Family Firm Institute.

Notes

1. In fact, many have misquoted Ward's statistics, indicating at each level that family firms survive "to" the next generation, rather than "through" that generation. This small change in preposition has large impact considering that a generation lasts 20 to 25 years.
2. This figure also represents the basic research framework of the STEP project, a global collaboration of more than 40 universities to explore entrepreneurship in the family context. The research framework has been developed jointly by researchers active in this project. For more information visit www.STEPProject.org.
3. We defined core company as the largest company within the family business group in terms of sales volume. There are family business groups that only consist of one company, which is then defined as the core company. This definition was provided in the introduction to the survey. Family business group in turn refers to the entirety of the business portfolio controlled by the business family. The family business group can consist of one or multiple companies.
4. We are indebted to Tom Lumpkin (Syracuse University), Michael Hitt (Texas A&M University), Per Davidsson (Queensland University of Technology), and Candida Brush (Babson College) for the guidance in the scale-building process.

References

Ahuja, G., & Lampert, C. M. (2001). Entrepreneurship in the large corporation: A longitudinal study of how established firms create breakthrough inventions. *Strategic Management Journal, 22*, 521–543.

Albert, S., & Whetten, D. A. (1985). Organizational identity. In L. L. Cummings & B. M. Staw (Eds.), *Research in organizational behavior* (Vol. 7, pp. 263–295). Greenwich, CT: JAI Press.

Anderson, R. C., & Reeb, D. M. (2003). Founding-family ownership and firm performance: Evidence from the S&P 500. *Journal of Finance, 58*, 1301–1328.

Andriopoulos, C., & Lewis, M. (2009). Exploitation-exploration tensions and organizational ambidexterity: Managing paradoxes of innovation. *Organization Science, 20*, 696–717.

Aronoff, C. (2001, August). Understanding family-business survival statistics. *Supply House Times, 44*(5), 34. Retrieved from http://www.supplyht.com/Articles/Feature_Article/09e3d1443c278010VgnVCM100000f932a8c0.

Arregle, J.-L., Hitt, M. A., Sirmon, D. G., & Very, P. (2007). The development of organizational social capital: Attributes of family firms. *Journal of Management Studies, 44*, 73–95.

Astrachan, J. H. (2010). Introduction to Volume 1. *Journal of Family Business Strategy, 1*, 1–5.

Audretsch, D. (1991). New firm survival and the technological regime. *Review of Economics and Statistics, 68*, 520–526.

Basco, R., & Perez-Rodriguez, M. J. (2009). Studying the family enterprise holistically. *Family Business Review, 22*, 82–95.

Berger, P. L., & Luckmann, T. (1966). *The social construction of reality: A treatise in the sociology of knowledge.* Garden City, NY: Doubleday.

Birley, S. & Westhead, P. (1994). A comparison of new businesses established by "novice" and "habitual" founders in Great Britain. *International Small Business Journal, 12*, 38–60.

Bourdieu, P. (1996). On the family as a realized category. *Theory, Culture & Society, 13*(3), 19–26.

Carter, S., & Ram, M. (2003). Reassessing portfolio entrepreneurship. *Small Business Economics, 21*, 371–380.

Chrisman, J. J., Chua, J. H., & Litz, R. A. (2004). Comparing the agency costs of family and non-family firms: Conceptual issues and exploratory evidence. *Entrepreneurship Theory and Practice, 28*, 335–354.

Chrisman, J. J., Chua, J. H., & Sharma, P. (2005). Trends and directions in the development of a strategic management theory of the family firm. *Entrepreneurship Theory and Practice, 29*, 555–575.

Chua, J. H., Chrisman, J. J., Kellermanns, F., & Wu, Z. (in press). Family involvement and new venture debt financing. *Journal of Business Venturing.* doi:10.1016/j.jbusvent.2009.11.002

Chua, J. H., Chrisman, J. J., & Sharma, P. (1999). Defining the family business by behavior. *Entrepreneurship Theory and Practice, 23*(4), 19–39.

Churchill, G. A. (1979). A paradigm for developing better measures of marketing constructs. *Journal of Marketing Research*, *16*, 64–73.

Covin, J. G., & Slevin, D. P. (1991). A conceptual model of entrepreneurship as firm behavior. *Entrepreneurship Theory and Practice*, *16*(1), 7–24.

Craig, J., & Moores, K. (2006). A 10-year longitudinal investigation of strategy, systems, and environment on innovation in family firms. *Family Business Review*, *19*, 1–11.

Cruz, C. C., Gomez-Mejia, L. R., & Becerra, M. (2010). Perceptions of benevolence and the design of agency contracts: CEO-TMT relationships in family firms. *Academy of Management Journal*, *53*, 69–89.

Cyert, R. M., & March, J. G. (1963). *A behavioral theory of the firm*. Englewood Cliffs, NJ: Prentice Hall.

Daily, C. M., & Dollinger, M. J. (1992). An empirical examination of ownership structure and family and professionally managed firms. *Family Business Review*, *5*, 117–136.

Danes, S. M., Stafford, K., Haynes, G., & Amarapurkar, S. S. (2009). Family capital of family firms: Bridging human, social, and financial capital. *Family Business Review*, *22*, 199–216.

Davidsson, P., & Wiklund, J. (2001). Levels of analysis in entrepreneurship research: Current research practice and suggestions for the future. *Entrepreneurship Theory and Practice*, *25*(4), 81–99.

Dess, G. G., Ireland, R. D., Zahra, S. A., Floyd, S. W., Janney, J. J., & Lane, P. J. (2003). Emerging issues in corporate entrepreneurship. *Journal of Management*, *29*, 351–378.

DeTienne, D. R. (2010). Entrepreneurial exit as a critical component of the entrepreneurial process: Theoretical development. *Journal of Business Venturing*, *25*, 203–215.

Donckels, R., & Fröhlich, E. (1991). Are family businesses really different? European experiences from STRATOS. *Family Business Review*, *4*, 149–160.

Dyer, W. G. (2003). The family: The missing variable in organizational research. *Entrepreneurship Theory and Practice*, *27*, 401–416.

Dyer, W. G., & Whetten, D. A. (2006). Family firms and social responsibility: Preliminary evidence from the S&P 500. *Entrepreneurship Theory and Practice*, *30*, 785–802.

Eddleston, K. A., & Kellermanns, F. W. (2007). Destructive and productive family relationships: A stewardship theory perspective. *Journal of Business Venturing*, *22*, 545–565.

Eddleston, K. A., Kellermanns, F. W., & Sarathy, R. (2008). Resource configuration in family firms: Linking resources, strategic planning and technological opportunities to performance. *Journal of Management Studies*, *45*, 26–50.

Eddleston, K. A., Kellermanns, F. W., & Zellweger, T. M. (2010). Exploring the entrepreneurial behavior of family firms: Does the stewardship perspective explain differences? *Entrepreneurship Theory and Practice*. Advance online publication. doi:10.1111/j.1540–6520.2010.00402.x

Eisenhardt, K. M. (2000). Paradox, spirals, ambivalence: The new language of change and pluralism. *Academy of Management Review, 25*, 703–705.

Faccio, M., & Lang, L. H. P. (2002). The ultimate ownership of Western European corporations. *Journal of Financial Economics, 65*, 365–395.

Frank, H., Lueger, M., Nose, L., & Suchy, D. (2010). The concept of "Familiness": Literature review and systems theory-based reflections. *Journal of Family Business Strategy, 1*, 119–130.

Fukuyama, F. (1995). *Trust*. New York, NY: Free Press.

Gavetti, G., & Levinthal, D. (2000). Looking forward and looking backward: Cognitive and experiential search. *Administrative Science Quarterly, 45*, 113–137.

Gedajlovic, E., Carney, M., Chrisman, J., & Kellermanns, F. (2011, February 1). The adolescence of family firm research: Taking stock and planning for the future (Working Paper). Vancouver, British Columbia, Canada: Simon Fraser University.

Gibson, C. B., & Birkinshaw, J. (2004). The antecedents, consequences, and mediating role of organizational ambidexterity. *Academy of Management Journal, 47*, 209–226.

Gomez-Mejia, L. R., Haynes, K. T., Nunez-Nickel, M., Jacobson, K. J. L., & Moyano-Fuentes, J. (2007). Socio-emotional wealth and business risks in family-controlled firms: Evidence from Spanish olive oil mills. *Administrative Science Quarterly, 52*, 106–137.

Gordon, G., & Nicholson, N. (2008). *Family wars: Classic conflicts in family business and how to deal with them*. London, England: Kogan Page.

Habbershon, T., Nordqvist, M., & Zellweger, T. (2010). Transgenerational entrepreneurship. In M. Nordqvist & T. Zellweger (Eds.), *Transgenerational entrepreneurship: Exploring growth and performance in family firms across generations* (pp. 1–38). Cheltenham, England: Edward Elgar.

Habbershon, T. G., & Pistrui, J. (2002). Enterprising families domain: Family-influenced ownership groups in pursuit of transgenerational wealth. *Family Business Review, 15*, 223–237.

Habbershon, T. G., Williams, M., & MacMillan, I. C. (2003). A unified systems perspective of family firm performance. *Journal of Business Venturing, 18*, 451–465.

Habbershon, T. G., & Williams, M. L. (1999). A resource-based framework for assessing the strategic advantages of family firms. *Family Business Review, 12*, 1–25.

He, Z., & Wong, P. (2004). Exploration vs. exploitation: An empirical test of the ambidexterity hypothesis. *Organization Science, 15*, 481–494.

Hinkin, T. R. (1995). A review of scale development practices in the study of organizations. *Journal of Management, 21*, 967–988.

Jennings, W. W., Horan, S. M., Reichenstein, W., & Brunel, J. L. P. (2011). Perspectives from the literature of private wealth management. *Journal of Wealth Management, 14*(1), 8–40.

Kellermanns, F. W., & Eddleston, K. A. (2006). Corporate entrepreneurship in family firms: A family perspective. *Entrepreneurship Theory and Practice, 30*, 809–830.

Le Breton-Miller, I., Miller, D., & Steier, L. P. (2004). Toward an integrative model of effective FOB succession. *Entrepreneurship Theory and Practice, 28*, 305–328.

Levinson, H. (1971). Conflicts that plague family businesses. *Harvard Business Review, 49*(2), 90–98.

Lewis, M. (2000). Exploring paradox: Toward a more comprehensive guide. *Academy of Management Review, 25*, 760–776.

Litz, R. A. (2008). Two sides of a one-sided phenomenon: Conceptualizing the family business and business family as a Mobius Strip. *Family Business Review, 21*, 217–236.

Liu, L. A., Chua, C. H., & Stahl, G. K. (2010). Quality of communication experience: Definition, measurement, and implications for intercultural negotiations. *Journal of Applied Psychology, 95*, 469–487.

Low, M. B., & MacMillan, I. C. (1988). Entrepreneurship: Past research and future challenges. *Journal of Management, 14*, 139–161.

Luhmann, N. (1984). *Soziale Systeme. Grundriß einer allgemeinen Theorie* [Social systems. Outline of a General Theory] (4th ed.). Frankfurt am Main, Germany: Suhrkamp.

Lumpkin, G. T., Brigham, K. H., & Moss, T. W. (2010). Long-term orientation: Implications for the entrepreneurial orientation and performance of family businesses. *Entrepreneurship & Regional Development, 22*(3), 1–24.

Lumpkin, G. T., & Dess, G. G. (1996). Clarifying the entrepreneurial orientation construct and linking it to performance. *Academy of Management Review, 21*, 135–172.

Lumpkin, G. T., Martin, W., & Vaughn, M. (2008). Family orientation: Individual-level influences on family firm outcomes. *Family Business Review, 21*, 127–138.

March, J. G. (1991). Exploration and exploitation in organizational learning. *Organization Science, 1*, 71–87.

Martin, L., & Lumpkin, T. (2003). *From EO to "family orientation": Generational differences in the management of family businesses.* Paper presented at the 22nd Babson College Entrepreneurship Research Conference, Babson Park, MA.

Mason, C. M., & Harrison, R. T. (2006). After the exit: Acquisitions, entrepreneurial recycling, and regional economic development. *Regional Studies, 40,* 55–73.

McConaugby, D. L., Matthews, C. H., & Fialko, A. S. (2001). Founding family controlled firms: Performance, risk, and value. *Journal of Small Business Management, 39,* 31–49.

Miller, D. (1983). The correlates of entrepreneurship in three types of firms. *Management Science, 29,* 770–791.

Moores, K. (2009). Paradigms and theory building in the domain of business families. *Family Business Review, 22,* 167–180.

Morck, R., Shleifer, A., & Vishny, R. W. (1988). Management ownership and market valuation: An empirical analysis. *Journal of Financial Economics, 20,* 293–315.

Morck, R., & Yeung, B. (2003). Agency problems in large family business groups. *Entrepreneurship Theory and Practice, 27,* 367–382.

Naldi, L., Nordqvist, M., Sjöberg, K., & Wiklund, J. (2007). Entrepreneurial orientation, risk taking, and performance in family firms. *Family Business Review, 20,* 33–47.

Naldi, L., Nordqvist, M., & Zellweger, T. M. (2011, August). Knowledge resources and performance: The moderating role of family involvement in strategy processes. Paper presented at the Academy of Management 2011 Annual Meeting, San Antonio, TX.

Nordqvist, M., Habbershon, T. G., & Melin, L. (2008). Transgenerational entrepreneurship: Exploring EO in family firms. In H. Landström, H. Crijns, & E. Laveren (Eds.), *Entrepreneurship, sustainable growth and performance: Frontiers in European entrepreneurship research* (pp. 93–116). Cheltenham, England: Edward Elgar.

Nordqvist, M., & Melin, L. (2010). Entrepreneurial families and family firms. *Entrepreneurship & Regional Development, 22*(3), 1–29.

Nordqvist, M., & Zellweger, T. (Eds.). (2010). *Transgenerational entrepreneurship: Exploring growth and performance in family firms across generations.* Cheltenham, England: Edward Elgar.

Pearson, A. W., Carr, J. C., & Shaw, J. C. (2008). Toward a theory of familiness: A social capital perspective. *Entrepreneurship Theory and Practice, 32,* 949–969.

Plate, M., Schiede, C., & von Schlippe, A. (2010). Portfolio entrepreneurship in the context of family owned businesses. In M. Nordqvist & T. Zellweger (Eds.), *Transgenerational entrepreneurship: Exploring growth and performance of family firms across generations* (pp. 96–123). Cheltenham, England: Edward Elgar.

Raisch, S., & Birkinshaw, J. (2008). Organizational ambidexterity: Antecedents, outcomes and moderators. *Journal of Management, 34,* 375–409.

Rauch, A., Wiklund, J., Lumpkin, G. T., & Frese, M. (2009). Entrepreneurial orientation and business performance: An assessment of past research and suggestions for the future. *Entrepreneurship Theory and Practice, 33*, 761–787.

Schulze, W. S., Lubatkin, M. H., & Dino, R. N. (2003). Toward a theory of agency and altruism in family firms. *Journal of Business Venturing, 18*, 473–490.

Schuman, S., Stutz, S., & Ward, J. (2010). *Family business as paradox*. New York, NY: Palgrave.

Schumpeter, J. A. (1934). *The theory of economic development*. Cambridge, MA: Harvard University Press.

Schwab, D. (1980). Construct validity in organizational behavior. In B. Staw & L. L. Cummings (Eds.), *Research in organizational behavior* (pp. 3–43). Greenwich, CT: JAI Press.

Sharma P. (2008). Commentary: Familiness: Capital Stocks and Flows Between Family and Business. *Entrepreneurship Theory & Practice, 32*(6): 971–977.

Scott, M., & Rosa, P. (1996). Has firm level analysis reached its limits? Time for a rethink. *International Small Business Journal, 14*(4), 81–89.

Sharma, P., & Manikutty, S. (2005). Strategic divestments in family firms: Role of family structure and community culture. *Entrepreneurship Theory and Practice, 29*, 293–311.

Sharma, P., & Salvato, C. (in press). Exploiting and exploring new opportunities over life cycle stages of family firms. A commentary on "Knowledge combinations and the potential advantages of family firms in searching for opportunities," by Jim Fiet and Pankaj Patel. *Entrepreneurship Theory and Practice*.

Sieger, P., Zellweger, T., Nason, R., & Clinton, E. (in press). Portfolio entrepreneurship in family firms. *Strategic Entrepreneurship Journal*.

Simon, F. (2006). *Einführung in Systemtheorie und Konstruktivismus* [Introduction to Systems Theory and Constructivism]. Heidelberg, Germany: Carl Auer.

Sirmon, D. G., & Hitt, M. A. (2003). Managing resources: Linking unique resources, management, and wealth creation in family firms. *Entrepreneurship Theory and Practice, 27*, 339–358.

Smith, W. K., & Lewis, M. W. (2011). Toward a theory of paradox: A dynamic equilibrium model of organizing. *Academy of Management Review, 36*, 381–403.

Steier, L. (2007). New venture creation and organization: A familial sub-narrative. *Journal of Business Research, 60*, 1099–1107.

Stewart, A., & Hitt, M. A. (2010). The Yin and Yang of kinship and business: Complementary or contradictory forces? (And can we really say?). *Advances in Entrepreneurship, Firm Emergence and Growth, 12*, 243–276.

Tagiuri, R., & Davis, J. (1996). Bivalent attributes of the family firm. *Family Business Review, 9,* 199–208.

Uhlaner, L. M., Kellermanns, F. W., Eddleston, K. A., & Hoy, F. (in press). The entrepreneuring family: A new paradigm for family business research. *Small Business Economics.*

Ward, J. (1987). *Keeping the family business healthy.* San Francisco, CA: Jossey-Bass.

Westhead, P., & Wright, M. (1998). Novice, portfolio, and serial founders: Are they different? *Journal of Business Venturing, 13,* 173–204.

Yamakawa, Y., Peng, M. W., & Deeds, D. L. (2010, August). *How does experience of previous entrepreneurial failure impact future entrepreneurship?* Paper presented at the 2010 Academy of Management annual meeting, Montreal, Quebec, Canada.

Zahra, S. A. (1995). Corporate entrepreneurship and financial performance: The case of management leveraged buyouts. *Journal of Business Venturing, 10,* 225–247.

Zahra, S. A. (2003). International expansion of U.S. manufacturing family businesses: The effect of ownership and involvement. *Journal of Business Venturing, 18,* 495–512.

Zahra, S. A. (2005). Entrepreneurial risk taking in family firms. *Family Business Review, 18,* 23–40.

Zahra, S. A., & Covin, J. G. (1995). Contextual influences on the corporate entrepreneurship-performance relationship: A longitudinal analysis. *Journal of Business Venturing, 10,* 43–58.

Zahra, S. A., & Sharma, P. (2004). Family business research: A strategic reflection. *Family Business Review, 17,* 331–346.

Zellweger, T. (2007). Time horizon, costs of equity capital, and generic investment strategies of firms. *Family Business Review, 20,* 1–15.

Zellweger, T., Kellermanns, F., Chrisman, J., & Chua, J. (in press-a). Family control and family firm valuation by family CEOs: The importance of intentions for transgenerational control. *Organization Science.*

Zellweger, T., Nason, R., Nordqvist, M., & Brush, C. (in press-b). Why do family firms strive for nonfinancial goals? An organizational identity perspective. *Entrepreneurship Theory and Practice.*

Zellweger, T., & Sieger, P. (2010). Entrepreneurial orientation in long-lived family firms. *Small Business Economics.* Advance online publication. doi:10.1007/s11187-010-9267-6

Zellweger, T. M., & Nason, R. S. (2008). A stakeholder perspective on family firm performance. *Family Business Review, 21,* 203–216.

Biographies

Thomas Markus Zellweger holds the Family Business Chair at the University of St. Gallen, Switzerland, where he runs the School's Center for Family Business. He is an associate editor of *Journal of Family Business Strategy* and serves on the editorial board of *Family Business Review*.

Robert S. Nason is a PhD student in the Whitman School of Management at Syracuse University and is the former assistant director for the STEP Project at Babson College.

Mattias Nordqvist is the Hamrin International Professor of Family Business at Jönköping International Business School. He is also the associate dean for doctoral programs and codirector for Center for Family Enterprise and Ownership at Jönköping International Business School.

ASSESSMENT TEST 1

It is now time to test your knowledge using the interactive assessment tool available online at www.familyenterprisebook.com/self-assessments. Enter "familyenterprise" as your password to proceed with the individual assessment. Your responses will be automatically scored and, in the event that you have entered an incorrect response, the correct answer will be provided.

1. True or False: Family enterprise is the most common form of business entity in the world.

2. True or False: The government of the United States has adopted a definition of family enterprise for tax purposes.

3. True or False: The European Union has had a definition of family business since 1999.

4. True or False: An academic definition of family enterprise is an enterprise "in which multiple members of the same family are involved as major owners or managers, either contemporaneously or over time."

5. True or False: A definition of family enterprise developed by practitioners is "an economic venture in which two or more members of a family have an interest in ownership and a commitment to the continuation of the enterprise."

6. True or False: A business must have at least two generations to be considered a family enterprise.

7. True or False: Family, governance, and enterprise constitute the three core systems that characteristically inform family enterprises.

8. True or False: "The family business is a business governed and/or managed with the intention to shape and/or pursue the vision of the business held by a dominant coalition controlled by members of the same family or a small number of families in a manner that is potentially sustainable across generations of the family or families" is a definition developed by practitioners.

9. True or False: A commitment to the continuation of the family enterprise is central to a practitioner's understanding and definition of family enterprise.

10. True or False: In one definition, family involvement in ownership (FIO) and family involvement in management (FIM) are measured as the percentage of equity held by family members and the percentage of a firm's managers who are nonfamily members.

CHAPTER 2

Classic Systems of a Family Enterprise

The three systems that constitute a family enterprise are:

- The family system.
- The ownership system.
- The enterprise system.

The three systems are complex and interlocking.

The *family system* may be quite broad, and may include several generations, cousins as well as siblings, and blood relatives as well as in-laws. Moreover the definition of family is always expanding as new concepts of family emerge across time.

The *ownership system* may also be broad, extending to various reaches of the family, and including those who work in the enterprise and those who do not. The ownership group may also include non-family members, such as nonfamily investors in the enterprise or long-time employees and professional advisors who may have been given an ownership stake.

Family and non-family members may also be involved in the *enterprise system*, as employees, for example, sometimes including top management. Frequently there is a "nonfamily CEO" or "nonfamily CFO."

THE FAMILY SYSTEM

The family system is comprised of individuals, groups of individuals, two or more generations and possibly even several branches of the family.

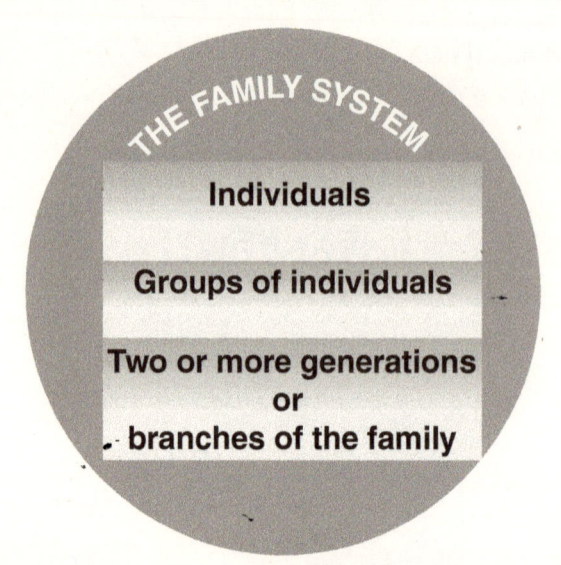

THE FAMILY SYSTEM
- Individuals
- Groups of individuals
- Two or more generations or branches of the family

But who, really, is in the family system? The answer to that question depends on how family is defined, but regardless of the operational definition of family, the family system will include individuals who have responsibilities, values, needs, and goals that may or may not be the same as the other individuals in the family system.

For example, an individual's connection to the enterprise may be direct in that he or she works in the business or has an ownership interest. That connection could also be indirect. For example, the individual may be married to or be a descendant of an owner or family member working in the enterprise.

The family system is also made up of groups of individuals, such as parents, children, couples, siblings, cousins, in-laws, and so on. And, in most cases, generations or branches of the family will typically be present in the family system.

THE OWNERSHIP SYSTEM

The ownership system is comprised of family, individuals, including existing and successor generations, family branches, nonfamily managers, employees, investors, trustees of trusts, shareholders, and/or individuals or companies.

In many cases, rights and duties of shareholders and family are often different and sometimes even conflicting.

Who, then, is in the ownership system? In a family enterprise, the ownership system usually consists of one or more subsets of the family system. However, owners can be individuals or entities (such as other businesses or trusts). Owners can include family and nonfamily (such as nonfamily managers, employees, investors, and/or trustees of trusts).

Ownership can also be organized by the subgroups that exist within the family, such as senior generations and successor generations and family branches. At the start, the founder may own all the stock; later stock ownership may be broadened to include other family members, who have varied interests in the enterprise. Often, ownership of a family enterprise remains largely or entirely in the hands of family members, passed down from generation to generation.

Another term referring to ownership is *shareholder*. A shareholder is an individual or a company that legally owns one or more shares of stock in a corporation. An enterprise can have only one shareholder, or it can have millions. In many family enterprises, a great deal of overlap occurs between the shareholders and the family.

Understanding the responsibilities, rights and duties of owners/shareholders under applicable law and agreements is necessary to understand how owners serve a different role from those who are considered "family." The family system itself, for example, has no legal responsibilities and rights regarding the enterprise except those that individual family members have if they are owners. For instance, owners may be required to guarantee loans to the enterprise to facilitate credit for the business while family members who are not owners are not usually asked to provide such guarantees.

It is important to be aware that the ownership system does not operate in a vacuum and can be influenced by a number of nonowners, such as nonfamily employees, advisors, spouses, and family members.

THE ENTERPRISE SYSTEM

The enterprise system includes those who work in the business or the enterprise. Examples of enterprises owned by families include operating business(es), real estate (including vacation homes and other property), diversified wealth portfolio(s), family offices, and charitable foundations.

A family enterprise can consist of various assets or activities, such as the operating businesses, real estate entity or entities, or diversified wealth portfolios.

Another possible configuration is the operating business with a diversified wealth portfolio held for the benefit of the family. Sometimes the portfolio is part of a separate entity, often referred to as a family office.

Families may also create charitable foundations that they substantially control. They typically view these as their enterprise, and such foundations are subject to country regulatory systems.

Of course, if we expand our thinking about what defines a family enterprise, additional forms may be identified. Consider how politics or governmental power can constitute a form of family enterprise that survives from generation to generation—think of the British royal family, or the Kennedys or the Bushes in the United States, or the Gandhis in India. Parts of the entertainment industry can also become a family enterprise—consider the Barrymores, Coppolas, and Redgraves among movie dynasties. Yet in all cases what is crucial is that we recognize the interlocking features of family, ownership, and enterprise systems.

> **KEY POINT**
>
> Every family enterprise includes at least three systems, and an adequate understanding of each system is crucial to understanding family enterprises.

Classic Systems of a Family Enterprise

ASSESSMENT TEST 2

It is now time to test your knowledge using the interactive assessment tool available online at www.familyenterprisebook.com/self-assessments. Enter "familyenterprise" as your password to proceed with the individual assessment. Your responses will be automatically scored and, in the event that you have entered an incorrect response, the correct answer will be provided.

1. Choose all responses that apply: If one is a family member without an ownership interest, by law what are his/her rights, responsibilities, and authority in the family enterprise?
   - ☐ Approval of strategic plans.
   - ☐ Authority to approve dividends.
   - ☐ Responsible for attending management meetings.
   - ☐ Responsible for understanding the functions of the Board of Directors.
   - ☐ None of the above.

2. Choose all responses that apply: Owners of family enterprises:
   - ☐ Are the individuals or entities who own shares in the enterprise.
   - ☐ Can include family and nonfamily members, for example, managers, employees, investors, and trustees of trusts.
   - ☐ Can also reflect subgroups that exist within the family such as senior generation and successor generation, and family branches.
   - ☐ Are always members of the family system.
   - ☐ None of the above.

3. Choose all the responses that apply: The family system includes:
   - ☐ Individuals.
   - ☐ Groups such as parents, children, siblings, cousins, in-laws, and so on.
   - ☐ Owners and/or nonowners.
   - ☐ Family members who may or may not work in the enterprise.
   - ☐ None of the above.

4. Choose all the responses that apply: The enterprise system:
   - ☐ Involves the interaction of all the systems involved with the enterprise.
   - ☐ Is made up only of groups of individuals.
   - ☐ Includes only family owners.
   - ☐ Is comprised of family and nonfamily.
   - ☐ None of the above.

5. Choose all the responses that apply: Which of the following could be considered a family enterprise?
   ☐ Operating businesses.
   ☐ Diversified wealth portfolios.
   ☐ Real estate.
   ☐ None of the above.

6. True or False: Family, owner, and enterprise systems are common to all family enterprises.

7. True or False: Often a diversified wealth portfolio is part of a separate entity called the family office.

8. True or False: What is important is to remember that the various systems in a family enterprise operate separately and apart from each other.

9. True or False: Nonfamily owners have the same rights and responsibilities as owners as do the family owners.

10. True or False: In a family enterprise, one of the main challenges is the conflicting rights and duties of the roles of family and owners.

CHAPTER 3

Representative Governance Systems in Family Enterprises

Governance

© Dennis Jaffe. Adapted from presentation.

Governance is the method or system of defining and enforcing the rights and responsibilities of a family enterprise with its various participants, including owners, managers, and family. Through effective governance, a family enterprise sets its direction, has consistent policies that the members of the enterprise agree to work by, and enforces the values that are part of the enterprise.

Besides the specific processes, customs, and policies that affect the family enterprise, governance also includes the relationships and decision rights among the parties involved in the enterprise.

45

These parties can be diverse, and include shareholders, management, board of directors, employees, suppliers, customers, banks and other lenders, regulators, the government, and the community. With effective governance of a family enterprise, the framework of rules and practices put in place ensures accountability, fairness, and transparency in the firm's relationship with all the parties.

ENTERPRISE GOVERNANCE

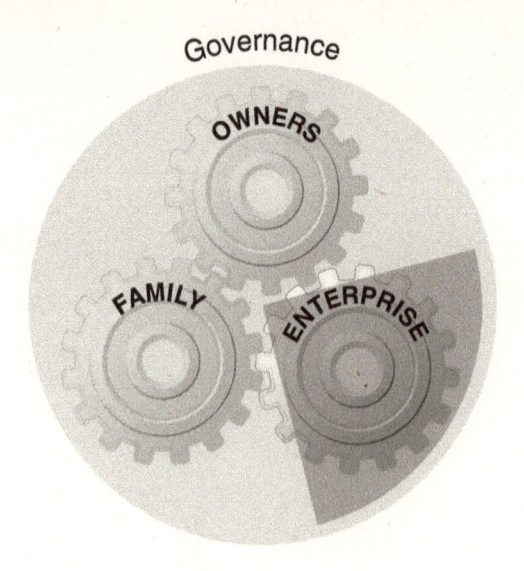

© Dennis Jaffe. Adapted from presentation.

Enterprises tend to change over time. Examples include the following:

- Individual entrepreneur: The founder creates an enterprise with most major decisions being made informally.
- Partnership: Sometimes the ownership is shared and formalized in a partnership, such as spouses or two siblings. Or a partnership may be created later, when other key family (or nonfamily) members are brought in.
- Corporation: It is likely that at some point a corporation, or other formal structure, will be formed. Corporations are created to limit the entity's

liability of assets and to provide a governance system and sometimes to invite participation by investors.
- Shareholders: A typical corporation is owned by its shareholders who select a board of directors, who, in turn, set major policies and select top management. In the early stages of a family enterprise, the various roles and responsibilities may be ignored, with few or no meetings of a board of directors. But at some point in its growth, the enterprise is likely to observe the legal forms in fact as well as in name. This change is often referred to as "professionalizing the family enterprise."
- Board of advisors (informal and formal): The family lawyer, accountant, trusted colleagues, or consultant may form a circle of informal advisors from the start of an enterprise. As the business matures, a board of advisors will often exclude professional advisors and move toward a more diverse membership. The board of advisors has no fiduciary responsibility and no formal power to make decisions but is available to the founder for advice from time to time.
- Board of directors: This is required in a corporate structure, and brings with it legal responsibilities and duties. Initially, the board may exist in name only, or be comprised solely of family members, but later as the enterprise is professionalized, a functioning board may be established with both family and independent directors. The board's functions are to represent the interests of the shareholders and to hold management accountable for the success of the enterprise by setting long-range policy and selecting and setting compensation for top management.

All of the preceding components of governance tend to be evolutionary in a family enterprise and evolve over a long period of time to deal with growth, change, and expansion of the family and enterprise network.

FAMILY GOVERNANCE: FAMILY COUNCIL

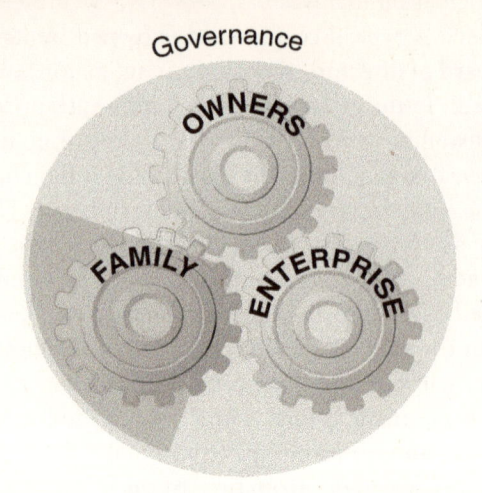

© Dennis Jaffe. Adapted from presentation.

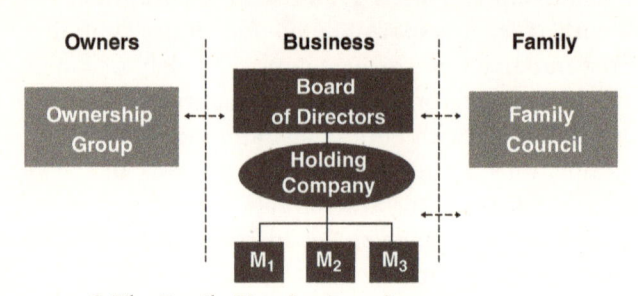

© The Family Firm Institute, Inc.

Families increasingly form family councils in businesses of all sizes and age. The family council is a way for all family members to learn about the enterprise firsthand.

The family council's main responsibility is to be the family's voice to the board of directors and to build effective communication and consensus among family members. Typically the family council is comprised of family members only, whether or not they are owners.

Some common tasks for the family council might include:

- Helping family members identify their collective and individual values, needs, and goals.

Representative Governance Systems in Family Enterprises   49

- Developing the structures, policies, and procedures to regulate the family's interaction internally and with the business.
- Responding to requests made by the ownership group.
- Communicating the family's interests in the enterprise to ownership.
- Developing healthy and strong family relationships.
- Preparing responsible next-generation owners and family members.
- Providing education and development opportunities for family members.
- Coordinating family philanthropy and stewardship.

OWNER GOVERNANCE: OWNERSHIP FORUM

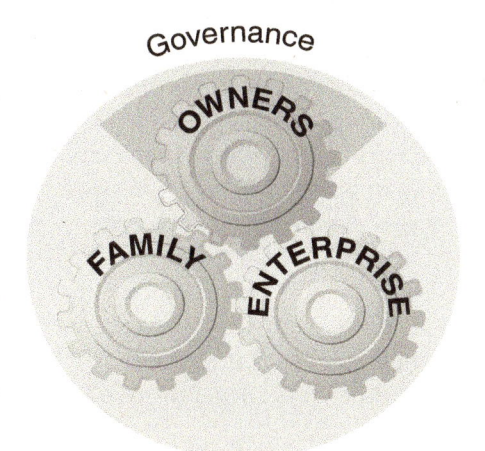

© Dennis Jaffe. Adapted from presentation.

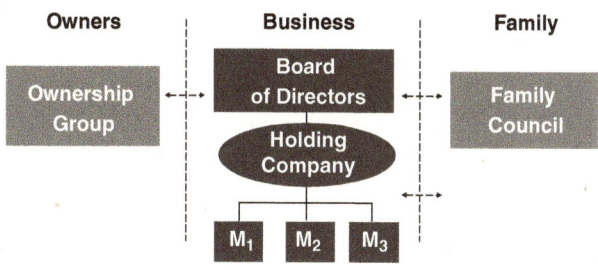

© The Family Firm Institute, Inc.

Often older and larger family enterprises form ownership forums to discuss issues specific to owners of the enterprise, including the direction

> **KEY POINT**
>
> Family enterprises have a variety of governance systems that typically encompass family, owners, and enterprise.

of the business, communications of the owners' requests to the board, owners' goals to the family, and building collaboration and consensus among the owners. The ownership forum, made up exclusively of owners, is another structure that helps to develop healthy boundaries between the systems.

Some common tasks for the ownership forum might include:

- Developing structure, policies, and procedures specifically for owners, individually or as a group.
- Responding to requests from the board and family.
- Building collaboration and consensus among owners.
- Coordinating owners' directives and decisions.

In sum, governance in family enterprises must stretch across the family enterprise system to include enterprise governance, family governance, and owner governance. While the first of these tends to take many forms, family councils and ownership forums play a prominent role in the latter two forms of governance.

ASSESSMENT TEST 3

It is now time to test your knowledge using the interactive assessment tool available online at www.familyenterprisebook.com/self-assessments. Enter "familyenterprise" as your password to proceed with the individual assessment. Your responses will be automatically scored and, in the event that you have entered an incorrect response, the correct answer will be provided.

1. Choose all responses that apply: Which of the following would be a typical change to a governance system over time?
   ☐ Stock ownership is broadened.
   ☐ A partnership develops.

☐ A corporation is formed.
☐ The rules and regulations change to accommodate family dynamics.
☐ None of the above.

2. True or False: Governance in a family enterprise is comprised exclusively of family shareholders.

3. True or False: With effective governance, the family enterprise benefits from consistent policies to which both family and nonfamily members must adhere.

4. True or False: Corporations are created to manage large family enterprises with many members.

5. True or False: Professionalizing the family enterprise implies that there are nonfamily shareholders.

6. True or False: In the case of younger family enterprises, the board of directors often exists initially in name only.

7. True or False: The main responsibility of the family's council or governance structure is to manage the business.

8. True or False: The ownership forum helps to develop healthy boundaries between the systems by developing structures, policies, and procedures for owners.

9. True or False: Each system of the family enterprise ideally has its own governance system.

10. True or False: The function of the owners' forum is to communicate the family's interests in the enterprise to the ownership.

CHAPTER 4
Key Characteristics of Family Enterprises

Family firms have a wide and often diverging set of characteristics, but research in the field of family enterprise has demonstrated that, for all their differences, family businesses tend to share a core set of characteristics. Indeed, such characteristics can—and often do—play a major role in determining the success or failure of family enterprises throughout the world.

CHARACTERISTICS

Resiliency, optimism, and a penchant for long-term strategies have been identified as characteristics of family firms for decades. These are attributes that can assist family firms and the stability of family firms in the short and long run, and will have an effect on the worldwide economic picture over the long haul.

In fact, family businesses have good track records. According to research done in the mid-1980s, approximately 30 percent of all family firms survive to the second generation. More recent research, however, using entrepreneurial models, may result in different and more optimistic statistics relating to the family's longevity in business versus the business's longevity.

Family business does not correlate with "small or underperforming businesses." One-third of the S&P 500 companies are family firms and, according to *Business Week* and *The Journal of Finance*, they outperform the nonfamily firms. Some examples of large family enterprises include: Wal-Mart, Cargill, Ford Motor Company, Motorola, Nordstrom, News Corp, and Ferragamo.

Some of the success of family enterprises is attributed to their unique traits. These include:

- Optimism: The majority of families who own family enterprises believe that the same family will control the family business in five years.
- Loyalty: Blood is thicker than water.

- Vigilance: No one watches your money like you do.
- Competitiveness: Scanning the market to see what competitors are doing and investing in IT, sales, and marketing. According to the 2007/2008 PricewaterhouseCoopers study, more than 86 percent of family businesses surveyed say that their top investment priority is IT infrastructure.
- Innovativeness: Although financially conservative, family businesses have shown the ability to discard the old and create new products and services. The reinvention of family firms is often vital to their survival.
- Nimbleness: Families that have lived and worked together for years can move quickly and are flexible in the many roles they play.
- Legacy and commitment: Families with names on the door report that their company is much more than just a job. It's their legacy, a commitment to the community and to the employees who work there and their families.

CHALLENGES

Of course, family enterprises also face unique challenges, including: conflicting goals and agendas in family, owners, and enterprise; several and often conflicting roles held by family members; and boundary management issues among the family, owners, and the enterprise.

Indeed, it must be emphasized that families in business together face many challenges, not the least of which is balancing the different and often conflicting agendas between family and business. Keeping family issues in the family and business issues in the business takes energy and time that are usually not required in nonfamily enterprises.

The relationships among parents and children, siblings, cousins, spouses, in-laws, and the myriad other family connections that are all part of a family enterprise circle make for a challenging and complex working environment.

Key Characteristics of Family Enterprises

The patterns of family dynamics are far more complex and deep-seated than patterns in a nonfamily business context; family behavior patterns develop and grow throughout a lifetime.

These patterns cause family enterprises to make decisions and develop strategies for the enterprise in different ways from nonfamily enterprises. One must tread carefully around the landmines of the family enterprise terrain.

Some specific challenges might include:

- Founders who often want their enterprise to continue after they die but resist formulating a succession plan.
- Family members who are not owners or involved in management (e.g., spouses, children, grandchildren) and yet believe they are entitled to provide input on issues affecting the enterprise. They can, and often do, exert significant informal influence and even control that can impact the enterprise at a conscious or unconscious level. Their participation may be positive and at the same time negative.
- The parent/child relationship. Parents often have a need to treat their children equally. One exception, although it is changing, is the rule of primogeniture (in other words, the custom of giving the eldest male beneficial treatment as it relates to the enterprise). Views of equality impact decisions about who will manage the enterprise, who can be owners, and who will receive other assets.

COMPARISON OF FAMILY SYSTEMS AND ENTERPRISE SYSTEMS

Indeed, the unique dynamics of a family enterprise arise as the enterprise and the family systems overlap one another over time. (See Table 4.1.)

Many of the conflicts, issues, and dilemmas facing families in business together are the result of differing values that are found between enterprises and families. A business primarily exists to increase shareholder wealth by being profitable and efficient.

Families, by contrast, exist to develop and support family members and to achieve strong bonds of emotional support. Individual members often wear two, sometimes three hats. The mother may be the CEO, mother, wife, and owner. Managing these roles is a constant challenge, especially when the goals and values of the business and family are at odds with each other.

TABLE 4.1 Comparisons of Family Systems and Enterprise Systems

Differences and Potential Areas of Conflict	Family Systems	Enterprise Systems
Goals	Development and support of family members	Profits, revenues, efficiency, growth
Relations	Deeply personal, of primary importance	Semipersonal or impersonal, of secondary importance
Rules	Informal expectations ("That's how we've always done it")	Written and formal rules, often with rewards and punishments spelled out
Evaluation	Members rewarded for who they are; effort counts; unconditional love and support	Support conditional on performance and results; employees can be promoted or fired
Succession	Caused by death or divorce	Caused by retirement, promotion, or departure
Authority	Based on family position or seniority	Based on formal position in the organization's hierarchy
Commitment	Intergenerational and lifetime; based on one's identity with the family	Short-term; based on rewards received for employment

Jane Hilburt-Davis and W. Gibb Dyer, Jr., *Consulting to Family Businesses* (San Francisco, CA: Jossey-Bass/Pfeiffer, 2003), 8.

Does she act in the role of CEO and fire her son who is not performing, or does she act as his mother and continue to support him?

In every case, what is crucial to remember is that family enterprises share a number of largely qualitative key characteristics. Far from existing as small underperforming businesses, family enterprises encompass a broad and large share of the global market, as family enterprises such as Wal-Mart and Ferragamo make abundantly clear. Yet regardless of size and market share, family enterprises face unique challenges and potential conflicts vis-à-vis individual perspectives and systems dynamics. Indeed, it is precisely for that reason that working with family enterprises requires a sophisticated understanding of the key characteristics of family enterprise and the challenges posed by family systems and enterprise systems.

> **KEY POINT**
>
> Coming to decisions in family enterprises often results in difficult and complex arrangements, due to differing perceptions of fairness, individual values, and long-range objectives. These differing perceptions can affect expectations, trust, communications, and family relationships.
>
> The unique dynamics of family enterprises arise as the family, ownership, enterprise, and governance systems overlap. The divergent values and functions are found at the intersection of these systems, and the challenge is to help the family enterprise manage the differences and conflicts and develop healthy boundaries between them.

ASSESSMENT TEST 4

It is now time to test your knowledge using the interactive assessment tool available online at www.familyenterprisebook.com/self-assessments. Enter "familyenterprise" as your password to proceed with the individual assessment. Your responses will be automatically scored and, in the event that you have entered an incorrect response, the correct answer will be provided.

1. Choose all responses that apply: What causes challenges peculiar to family enterprises?
   - ☐ Family dynamics.
   - ☐ Business management and ownership continuing in the family over generations.
   - ☐ The types of financing used in the business.
   - ☐ None of the above.

2. Choose all responses that apply: Which of the following is considered an area where problems occur in a family enterprise?
   - ☐ Unclear roles, responsibilities, and boundaries.
   - ☐ Competition of different values, needs, and goals.

☐ Uncertainty over who has what authority and who is accountable to whom.
☐ None of the above.

3. Choose all responses that apply: Which of the following is a characteristic common to family enterprises?
   ☐ Resiliency.
   ☐ Competitiveness.
   ☐ Impulsiveness.
   ☐ Innovativeness.
   ☐ None of the above.

4. Choose all responses that apply: The enterprise system:
   ☐ Involves the interaction of all the systems involved with the enterprise.
   ☐ Is made up only of groups of individuals.
   ☐ Includes only family owners.
   ☐ Is comprised of family and nonfamily.
   ☐ None of the above.

5. True or False: The family system is made up of family members and those nonfamily members who are owners.

6. True or False: You can assess the effectiveness (or ineffectiveness) of the groups by determining how everyone's values, needs, and goals are being met.

7. True or False: One of the challenges in family enterprises is that parents often have a need to treat their children equally and this impacts decisions about who will manage the enterprise, who can be owners, and who will receive other assets.

8. True or False: Working with family enterprises is often a challenge because of the unique dynamics of overlapping systems.

9. True or False: The historic rule of primogeniture refers to the custom of giving the eldest child (son or daughter) beneficial treatment as it relates to the enterprise.

10. True or False: The popular conception that most family businesses do not survive to the third generation has been challenged by newer statistics from the FFI/Goodman Study on Longevity, which shows family enterprise as much more enduring.

CHAPTER 5

Concepts in Family Enterprise Study

Among the many concepts used to understand family enterprises, two are crucial. The first concept is actually a series of applications from systems thinking—particularly the notion of seeing the family enterprise as a system of overlapping and interacting subsystems.

The second concept, that of process and content, involves recognizing the difference between the two and an examination of how each is used in working with and within family enterprises.

> **KEY POINT**
>
> Two concepts—that of systems thinking and process and content—are central to an adequate understanding of family enterprises.

SYSTEMS THINKING: A VERY BRIEF HISTORY

General systems theory has its roots in several fields including quantum physics, anthropology, biology, and mathematics. Family systems then built on and expanded general systems theory and began to blossom in the 1960s and 1970s.

Already in the mid–to–late 1950s, the family therapy systems movement—a system by which problems and solutions are viewed in the interaction between and among individuals—was adapted by several other fields, including seminarians, community organizers, psychologists, management, and organization development professionals. Across the board, the appeal of systems theory is its ability to be understood intuitively despite its intellectual complexity.

SYSTEMS THINKING: THE INDIVIDUAL IN THE SYSTEM

Systems thinking shifts the focus from the individual to the family enterprise as a system—a system with patterns of relationships involving roles, responsibilities, and goals. Because family enterprises are comprised of several overlapping systems (family, enterprise, ownership, governance, and generational) there are often conflicting goals and values. Individuals with a systems perspective appreciate that problems usually exist between people, not within them.

This perspective allows individuals to take the "high and long view," understanding that any change within a system has ripple effects and sometimes unintended consequences. Systems thinking is necessary for any change effort since either party to a relationship can change his or her part in the patterns at any time and, as a result, change the interactions. Any professional working with the family enterprise system will undoubtedly benefit from an understanding of systems thinking.

Systems Theory

Systems theory includes both open systems and closed systems.

Consider the following example of how a family system functions as an open system. A minor external economic event could cause an owner to panic, put the family company up for sale, causing turmoil and anxiety at the family and board levels. This can then cause shareholder values to nosedive and family stress to skyrocket.

Open systems interact with other systems constantly and change is therefore nonlinear and unpredictable. Nonlinear dynamics refers to systems where change is not in a straight line and is disorderly. Input is not necessarily proportional to output. Huge events can have a negligible effect and small events can have huge effects.

Closed systems, by contrast, have little or no interaction with other systems and they change in a linear, predictable way. For example, turning up the thermostat activates the furnace, and thus produces a clearly linear reaction.

> **KEY POINT**
>
> Family systems function as open systems, that is, as systems that interact with other systems in nonlinear and unpredictable ways.

RELEVANT SYSTEMS CONCEPTS: TRIANGLES, SCAPEGOAT(ING), HOMEOSTASIS, BOUNDARIES

Systems concepts are especially useful for clarifying and gaining a better understanding of the many interpersonal complexities of family enterprises. Indeed, three such concepts are of particular relevance here, namely, triangles, scapegoat(ing), and homeostasis.

Triangl(ing)

The term *triangles* (or *triangling* or *triangulation*) is used to describe the tendency of two people who are unable to resolve a conflict—or who are experiencing distress in their relationship—to involve a third person, entity, or process.

One obvious example of a triangle in family enterprise is two siblings who have a long–term conflicted relationship with one another and consistently involve a parent in their quarrels.

Triangling is a normal reaction and transient triangles exist in every family and business. Such triangles only become dysfunctional when the same people repeat the process for the same reasons over time.

Introducing a third person (or entity) can be a way of avoiding problems and of temporarily lowering intensity. Families that have a longstanding process of triangling instead of dealing with problems will not succeed in business, nor will they complete family tasks.

Another important lesson of long–standing triangles is that consultants can get pulled into triangles, especially in conflict–ridden families. One of the signals that the family business is trying to triangle a consultant and deflect the intensity of the change process appears when the consultant begins to have a difficult time being creative and getting perspective on the situation.

A ready example of this is when two siblings who have a long-term conflicted relationship with each other try to convince the consultant how right each one is and just how wrong the other is. In such cases, the best move the consultant can make is to address the triangling process and facilitate a dialogue between them that can help them work together more productively.

Scapegoat(ing)

Scapegoat(ing) is a familiar term. The word comes from the biblical ceremony in which the sins of the people were placed on the goat's head and the goat is sent into the wilderness. This word most commonly refers to the person or object that is blamed.

In family therapy, it is a term that often refers to the child unconsciously chosen by the parents to blame for the problems of the family. It is also often used to refer to the one in the work or family situation who "carries the symptoms" and the one most obviously affected by the conflicts and problems. The scapegoat often serves as a focal point for the anger in the family and the business. In some situations, the scapegoat may be an entity such as the business.

In family businesses, often the family is the scapegoat for all of the business problems, and professionals often accept that without challenging these assumptions. In such cases, the important questions to ask are: Does this person deserve the blame that is being put on him or her? Or, is scapegoat(ing) here just a distraction from the real problems? Are we "buying into" the family's blaming? Or, do we need to look deeper and reexamine our own assumptions and identify the real work to be done?

Homeostasis

Homeostasis refers to the ability of any living system to maintain a degree of stability while still being able to adapt and change. In the context of family enterprise, it is the family's ability to self-correct after a crisis and the business's ability to weather the ups and downs of the economy.

Think of homeostasis as the ability to change and yet remain stable. During times of crisis, living systems tend to move temporarily toward extremes of functioning. That is, they tend either to hunker down and keep the problem to themselves, or they may panic and call in many advisors haphazardly. As they readjust and adapt, they return to a new normal of stability. Flexibility, nimbleness, creativity, and patience are all characteristics of a system's ability to weather the storms of life. In family enterprises this flexibility is often seen as family members playing many roles, pitching in, working together when the going gets tough.

Boundaries

In the context of family enterprises, boundary functioning describes the quality of both the connection and the separation between the family and the enterprise.

For example, in a family enterprise facilitating healthy, regulated communications across boundaries, it is the family council's role to focus channeled communications to the board. In this case the boundary is not a barrier but rather akin to a healthy cell membrane. It is semi–permeable and regulates the exchange of substances, energy, information, emotions, and values between systems. It is through this regulated exchange that each system can grow and adapt, while at the same time maintain its own identity.

By contrast rigid and impervious boundaries cut off exchange, while diffusive boundaries fail to maintain a system's identity, often causing conflict and confusion.

CONTENT AND PROCESS

It would not be an exaggeration to say that professionals are always operating in two modes: content and process. But what is content? And, what is process?

Content is what is said or done. As the following article articulates, "Many attorneys, for example, have sophisticated skills for managing the communication and relationship issues involved in their work. They are likely to describe these skills as 'professional wisdom' or the 'art' of litigation rather than as process skills. They may be less likely than those from a management or behavioral sciences background to make them a focus of study and intervention."

Process is how something is said or done. Process includes the patterns of interactions among people in the present and over time, like the coach diagramming plays for a basketball team. Process questions might include: "We seem to be stuck on finding a solution to this. What do you think the reason might be?"

> **KEY POINT**
>
> Content is what is said or done, while process is how something is said or done.

Process also includes attention to nonverbal clues, like the way a phrase is spoken. Quoting from the article that follows, "... the emotional tone of an interchange, and the feel of what is happening. An owner–father says to his daughter, 'Yes, I really trust you to take over.' The tone of the statement defines the message. It can convey a supportive, caring message or a sarcastic put–down."

The ability to identify content and process is an art that develops over time. The correct ratio of one to the other can mean the difference between success and failure. And the overemphasis on one at the expense of the other is something to avoid. The ability to analyze the patterns of human interaction can provide leverage for changing dysfunctional and entrenched ways of operating or communicating. For example, it is often useful to look at how decisions are made—is the decision–making process unilateral, through consensus, or maybe by majority rule? Recognizing and pointing out these human processes will encourage improvements and can inspire a work culture that positively reinforces asking questions about assumptions.

Practitioners of negotiation and conflict resolution specialize in decision making about resources. They describe the two kinds of negotiation that take place simultaneously: one about the substantive issue and one about the rules for dealing with the issue. It is evident that these two negotiations correspond to content and process. Many costly legal battles are avoided by content–expert consultants who practice the art of tending carefully to resistance and emotions (the process) in dealing with difficult client situations.

The most effective advisor or consultant moves back and forth between process and content and knows which to emphasize when. This is especially necessary when working with family enterprises, which have a long–shared history, richly woven with love and problems, as well as a task to perform. The family enterprise advisor or consultant who doesn't integrate process and content leaves the family members the burden of doing this difficult work themselves.

A working example of this might be a transition process, such as succession. While managing succession, the consultant or advisor needs to gather data and know the current state to facilitate the process of the transition, while also understanding the financial and legal ramifications of such a change. Fair process is critical to family enterprise sustainability. Remember, when stuck in process, move to content (and vice versa). Also bear in mind that the older and more complex the issues, the higher the ratio of process to content at the outset.

You have now finished Chapter 5. Before doing the assessments, please read "Using the Process/Content Framework: Guidelines for the Content Expert" from *Family Business Review* that follows.

Using the Process/Content Framework: Guidelines for the Content Expert

Jane Hilburt-Davis, Key Resources, Cambridge, MA, USA
Peg Senturia, Family Therapist, Brookline, MA, USA

Abstract

Family business consultants, whatever their profession of origin, can make use of the distinction between what people say (content) and how they say it (process). This article summarizes some key concepts that process experts draw from family systems, organization development, and conflict resolution/negotiation theories to formulate a process/content framework. We suggest guidelines, illustrated with case examples, that can help family business consultants who are content experts move more thoughtfully and effectively between these two ways of viewing a family business. These guidelines can also help family businesses choose between the process or content experts they may need in different situations.

Introduction

All consultants, whatever their profession of origin, are always operating in two modes. In the content mode, they are working with their professional subject-matter expertise, such as tax planning or market research. In the process mode, they are creating and managing relationships with their clients and attending to the interpersonal impact of their interventions.

Professionals with process expertise, such as family therapists and organizational consultants, study both modes as part of their subject-matter expertise. They make the distinction between what people say (content) and how they say it (process). Content includes a specific body of knowledge. Process includes the relationship patterns within the client organization as well as between the clients and the consultants.

Professionals with content expertise, such as accountants, planners, and bankers, address both content and process but do not usually label them as such. Many attorneys, for example, acquire sophisticated skills for managing the communication and relationship issues involved in their work. They are likely to describe these skills as "professional wisdom" or the "art" of litigation rather than as process skills. They are less likely than family or organizational consultants to make them an explicit focus of study and intervention.

Traditionally, writers describe consultation frameworks in ways that sharply differentiate process experts and content experts. For example, Bork, Jaffe, Lane, and Heisler (1993) maintain that there are two main types of consultants, the process consultant and the expert consultant, although they do note that the adviser plays many different roles. Schein's vivid description of process consultation (Schein, 1988) establishes it conceptually as a distinct specialty.

Taking these conceptual distinctions too far can lead to trouble. As Whiteside and Brown suggest, "dichotomies are easily shifted into good versus bad and functional versus nonfunctional, with the family still tending to be considered the system that impedes the functioning of the business" (Whiteside and Brown, 1991, p. 385). This splitting can create professional stereotyping that slows the development of family business theory. Under this scenario, therapists take charge of the process, the emotions, the family; bankers, lawyers, and accountants take charge of the content, the business, the facts.

Without much stretch of the imagination, we can expect a concurrent splitting around traditional gender roles. Women, whatever their area of expertise, may be assigned the emotions, the "softer side" of the consultation; men are assumed to be better at the facts, the content side. This splitting around stereotypic gender roles, in fact, hinders the use of all the abilities of both men and women consultants. This is particularly important to avoid when working with family businesses in which, historically, women have often taken a back seat.

Based on our experience as both family therapists and organizational consultants, we think that focusing on only process expertise or only content expertise hinders the exciting integration of professional disciplines that is occurring in the study of family firms. We suggest that the family business consultant must know the difference between process and content, understand the importance of each, and use not just one or the other but carefully select from both modes, as circumstances indicate, to meet the unique needs of the family business.

Theoretical Background

Professionals define *process* in different ways. In family-systems theory, *process* refers to the patterns of interactions among people in the present and over time.

The family-systems therapist describing the process is like the football coach diagramming plays for a team. The therapist clarifies and articulates the process by observation and by asking such questions as: Who takes the initiative on what topics? Who typically opposes whom? Where are the alliances? How are roles played out?

Most family therapists also pay a lot of attention to emotional and other nonverbal aspects of communication. For them, process includes the way a phrase is spoken, the emotional tone of an interchange, the feel of what is happening. An owner-father says to his daughter, "Yes, I really trust you to take over." The tone of the statement defines the message. It can convey a supportive, caring message or a sarcastic put-down.

Family therapy relies heavily on a process-oriented theory of change. The therapist promotes lasting change in the family by helping the family change its patterns of interaction. This may include how family members communicate and how they make decisions, or the nature of key family relationships. In this sense, therapists use the concept of process to explain how significant change occurs (Watzlawick, Weakland, and Fisch, 1974).

In the language of business, *process* has a number of different meanings. A process engineer specializes in understanding the physical flow of a production line. In this sense a manufacturing process is usually concretely defined and documented. Total quality management speaks more generally about work processes in all areas of the organization, including white-collar jobs such as marketing or research. For example, marketing has a process for transforming manufacturing's product information into brochures that the sales force can use. Like family therapists, practitioners of quality management also have a theory of change built on describing and changing processes.

Other organizational theorists use *process* to emphasize the human side of work (Kanter, 1985). They are like family therapists who stress the emotional dimensions of communication. An overemphasis on this sense of process, at the expense of content, often evokes negative reactions in the business world, where people are usually expected to manage their feelings privately For example, Schaffer and Thomson criticize "touchy-feely" programs as "fundamentally flawed" and as confusing "ends with means, process with outcomes" (Schaffer and Thomson, 1992, p. 80).

Yet many business people know that analyzing the patterns of human interaction provides leverage for changing dysfunctional ways of operating. For example, it is often useful to look at a decision-making process, that is, how decisions are made, such as unilaterally, through consensus, or by majority rule. Looking at these human processes encourages improvements and supports a work culture that positively reinforces asking questions about assumptions.

Practitioners of negotiation and conflict resolution specialize in decision making about resources. They describe the two kinds of negotiation that take place simultaneously: one about the substantive issue and one about the rules for dealing with the issue. These two negotiations clearly correspond to content and process (Fisher and Ury, 1991).

Integrating Process and Content in Consultation

Content-expert consultants manage the process all the time but often without analyzing how they do it. The CPA who works with second-generation siblings in a potentially damaging business conflict not only deals with the financial issues but, through example, patience, and encouragement, also resolves the relationship issues (process side) of the dispute. Many costly legal battles are avoided by content-expert consultants who practice the art of tending carefully to resistance and emotions (the process) in dealing with difficult client situations.

In essence, every time the family business consultant (FBC) steps back by deliberately shifting attention from the content of a discussion (the what) to examine how things are happening, the consultant is looking at process. By looking at patterns in this larger arena, the consultant can discover, think about, and use more levers for intervention. Because process and content exist together, focusing on only one or the other means doing only part of the job. Obviously, the observer sees through a preferred lens, defined by values, training, experience, and profession of origin. However, the most effective consultant moves back and forth between process and content and knows which to emphasize when. This is especially necessary when working with family firms, who have a long-shared history, richly woven with love and problems, as well as a task to perform. The FBC who fails to integrate process and content leaves the family members the burden of doing this difficult work themselves.

The CPA, for example, needs a working knowledge of how to observe family patterns of behavior and communication (process). The family therapist, by the same standard, must be able to read a balance sheet (content). Each also needs to be sufficiently aware of his or her own limits to know when to call the other for help. The CPA can do as much damage trying to handle complex process issues as the family therapist can do trying to give sophisticated investment advice.

We will present seven guidelines, illustrated with case examples, for using our simple process/content framework. We have chosen two of the many situations in which the framework can be applied: managing communication and managing change. The first four guidelines follow a brief discussion of managing communication, and the last three guidelines follow a brief discussion of managing change.

We will also point out how the FBC can use the awareness of his or her own experience of the process as a signal about how to proceed with the consultation. Family therapists emphasize the importance of this kind of self-awareness because it is such a powerful tool in planning interventions.

Managing the Communication Process

Problems with communications can take many forms. Here are some examples:

"I have no idea what's happening with my sisters. How can we run the business this way?" "Dad won't discuss his succession plan." "We fight all the time."

Note that there is no such thing as "not communicating." Families are always communicating. A complaint that "my father won't communicate with me" really means that he doesn't communicate in ways I understand, approve of, or agree with.

Through the content lens, the consultant looks at what subjects the family members won't discuss or what information they lack. Through the process lens, the consultant looks at how the family patterns support the non-communication. Skills in both content and process are critical to effective communication. The goal is to keep the communication clear and direct and to put the content into words. What is not spoken in families can be much more powerful than what is spoken and dealt with directly.

Only by being aware of both process and content can the consultant gauge how well they are fitting together. In situations in which the nonverbal message and the verbal message have opposite meanings, communication is confusing, decisions are postponed, and plans for action are often derailed.

Guideline 1: Pay Attention to Your Internal Signals about the Congruence of Content and Process in Communications.

Incongruent messages are ones in which there is a discrepancy between the content and the process; the tone or context belies the message and confuses the receiver. Well-functioning families send congruent messages; dysfunctional families send incongruent messages. When the receiver cannot comment on the conflicting messages and perceives no way out, the message is called a double bind (Bateson, Jackson, Haley, and Weakland, 1968).

Think about the feelings you experience when you are getting a double-bind message. Such internal signals may include feeling confused and angry, feeling hopeless and helpless in a client situation that is usually simple for you, feeling anxious or overly involved with a client, or avoiding some clients by putting them last on your weekly schedule. You may see no way out and blame yourself. You may feel stonewalled and confused in a situation where you usually can find answers or at least know where to look. You are as befuddled as the son in the following old joke:

Mom gives her son two shirts for his birthday, one green and one blue. He wears the green one, and Mom says, "Oh, how nice, you're wearing your new shirt! What's the matter, you don't like the blue one?"

In complex, difficult situations where you have dealt effectively with the content and are still stymied, you can bring in a process expert, such as a family therapist, to work with you in resolving the issues.

Case Example. You are hired to help a family firm with a succession plan. The family just can't find the time to schedule meetings, although they keep telling you that they really want to do this. Their nonverbal and verbal messages are not sending the same information. The content (fact) is that their calendars are booked. You find, after asking about the history, that the process (pattern) is not new in this family. That discovery leads to a temporary shift in the problem definition from succession planning to how they keep from finding the time to meet.

Guideline 2: Give Your Expert Opinion When the Time Is Right; Know the Signals That the Family Is Not Ready to Listen.

Family firms often hire consultants for their content expertise and then ignore their advice. It is critical that you be aware of the subtle and not-so-subtle signals from the family firm members that you are moving too fast for them. These signs include repeating questions, making sarcastic comments, canceling meetings, making excuses for not getting the work done, and avoiding or blaming other family members. Don't be afraid of using your feelings as data. If you sense that the family is not ready for an expert opinion, focus on the process.

Case Example. You are called in by the founder to design a gifting program. You have already had two meetings with him and his wife. Because he has not done any of the homework you assigned and asks you the same questions in each meeting, you decide to move from content to process. You ask about how this plan affects him, not what he's going to do. You find out what giving to his children means to him and his wife and what their hopes and goals are for the business and family. Eventually you see clear signals that they are ready to put a plan into action: they do their homework, they are able to organize the information, and they let you know that they have resolved their concerns. Then you move to content and draw up a plan with them.

Guideline 3: Be Aware of Your Own Needs and Issues So You Can Separate Them from Your Clients' Needs and Issues.

The blending of emotional complexity and work goals in family firms challenges the consultant's objectivity. The clearer you are about your own role in working with the family business, the more comfortable you can be in shifting between content and process. Because socializing with clients increases the emotional complexity of the relationships, consultants who focus more on emotional processes usually want to maintain more social distance. To manage your involvement with clients to ensure their best interests, you need to keep clear about your role and honest about your agenda. Your opinions and feelings derived from your personal history must be put aside so that you can help your clients to find solutions that are best for them.

Case Example. You are a lawyer called by two sons and the daughter of a family business. Their concern is how their father-founder wants to treat his four children. These three have worked very hard in the business to keep it successful. The fourth is unemployed, lives with his parents, and has chosen not to be involved with the family business. He has never held a job for very long, and it doesn't seem that he will ever be self-sufficient. Now the parents insist that he receive a larger gift each year because "he is needier than the others, and they have the business."

You recognize a danger signal. This situation is close to your own: your parents have given the "black sheep" in your family (your younger brother) much more than you or your older sister because "he needs it more." You realize that you must be careful to separate your feelings from your clients' needs.

You prepare yourself to deal with these emotionally charged process issues. You begin with the content by educating your clients on the facts and helping them sort out what is best for the family and the firm. You watch for signals to shift to process issues. The parents are clear about their wishes and are ready to get on with the agreement. Using your feelings as data allows you to step back and realize that your desire to focus on the process is really your own need to work through your feelings about your younger brother. These feelings can range from anger to confusion to over-involvement that seem to be out of proportion to the situation. These clients are not the ones who need to work more on process in this situation!

Guideline 4: When Dealing with Conflict, Help the Family Stay on Task by Addressing the Underlying Issues.

Relatives rarely fight openly about what they are really fighting about. Fights or arguments usually go on at one content level and mean something else, especially in families with a long history of bickering. The conflict will continue to recycle if the underlying process issues are not identified, examined, and resolved. In this situation, exploring the process is a necessary detour that leads from an impasse to a way out. Mediation theories of conflict resolution put the mediator in charge of managing the process and leave the interested parties in charge of the content or outcome (Moore, 1986).

> *Case Example. You have almost finished helping set up a family council. You cannot figure out why two of the adult siblings continue to fight about seemingly insignificant details. This signals you to look for a process issue. You sit down with both of them to figure out what this fight is really about. You discover that it has its origins in resentment about job assignments made ten years ago and never discussed between them. As you get them to talk about it, you make analyzing the process of their underground fight the content for the consultation. This helps them to see that clearing the air, even after all these years, enables them to get on with their business. In this intervention, you model positive ways of resolving disagreements and reinforce direct communication skills.*

Managing the Change Process

Next we review issues in managing change and then use examples from this area to illustrate the last three guidelines for using the process-content framework.

Family firms may need help with an internal, planned change, such as succession, leadership, or diversification; with an external change such as increased competition or new tax laws; or with an internal, unplanned change that should have been anticipated, such as death, divorce, or children wanting out of the business.

To help the family business manage change and solve the new problems that accompany it, the FBC must first determine whether the situation presents a content problem or a process problem. Content problems usually require a first-order change, that is, change within the rules of the family business.

Process problems often require second-order change, that is, change outside the rules (Watzlawick, Weakland, and Fisch, 1974). This type of change and learning means using a process lens to examine the problem and to generate breakthroughs. It requires stepping back to question the accepted rules by identifying and questioning unspoken assumptions. It takes decreasing the defensiveness in individuals and groups so that learning can occur.

Change involves both solving the problem at hand (content, first-order change) and learning how to solve problems in general (process, second-order change). Senge, in his study of change in organizations, emphasizes the key role of learning (Senge, 1991). Argyris (1991, p. 100) notes that "people define learning too narrowly as mere 'problem solving' so they focus on identifying and correcting errors in the external environment" instead of learning to solve problems in general.

Guideline 5: Create a Safe Environment for New Learning.

Your job as a consultant includes creating a "safety zone" for the family business during change. The right amount of safety is necessary for learning. If people are too comfortable or too nervous, they will not be open to new information. Attending to both content and process helps to build this safe environment. Give expert opinions on content, keep the group on track, and check the process regularly. Signals to shift from content to process include increased and repetitious conflict about the same or similar issues, denial of the reality of change, and deteriorating personal interactions, such as scapegoating and sarcasm. Signals to shift from process to content include clear and direct communication, agreement that each individual has had a chance to be heard and is ready to solve the problem of the moment, and a sense that it is time to get down to business and take action.

Here are some tips for creating safety for the family firm during transitions:

- Begin and end meetings on time.
- Give everyone a chance to be heard.
- Help individuals get their questions answered.
- Monitor interactions so that no one speaks for anyone else.
- Keep surprises to a minimum.
- Help the family create a vision of the future.
- Establish a family council or another form of regular family meetings.

Case Example: You get a call from a sixty-seven-year-old woman whose husband died three months ago. He was the founder of a small but thriving food service business. She and her husband had planned to retire soon and give the business to their two sons. But they had made no formal arrangements, *and now she is confused about where to begin. She has always worked part-time in the business, but only as she could fit it in. Sometimes she and her sons have disagreed about how much she should be involved. Although she has usually trusted her sons' judgment, she knows that she needs some professional help in protecting her own and the business's interests.*

The initial evaluation shows that these are people who have kept their family strong and their business growing over the years. In the past their processes, including how they communicated, resolved conflicts, and solved problems, worked. Now, with the father gone, the mother fears facing retirement alone and the sons are uncertain about their new roles. One of your first interventions is to create safety by establishing regular family meetings to develop a joint strategy for the business while attending to their personal concerns. At this time of change, they need content expertise, such as information about transferring ownership. You also use their need to create new processes in the absence of the founder to help them learn how to master this new stage of life.

Guideline 6: Respect Resistance to Change

Too often we think of resistance as a destructive fire to be stamped out. It is better to see it as the family firm's coat of armor, protecting it from a change that seems overwhelming. Sometimes the family even wears it to protect itself from consultants who have assessed the situation incorrectly or who are moving too quickly. Resistance cannot be ignored. In fact, it should be treated with respect. It is a protective mechanism for any system, as well as a functional barrier to the absorption of new information.

Enlist the family in identifying and understanding the resistance. Encourage family members to get into a reflective mode so that they can recognize responses that are counterproductive. Reflective thinking means looking at the process and identifying what is right and wrong with the way they are managing change. Help them step back and look at the situation objectively. Ury refers to this as "going to the balcony" (1993, p. 38). By shifting from the content lens to the process lens, the family members and the consultant can identify where the resistance is and what it is protecting. Help them identify family patterns that are ineffective. Identify any members who may be gaining from resisting the change. Instead of fighting change, the family can use the new information about themselves and the business to function more productively.

At the same time, carefully monitor your own feelings for danger signals about the family's resistance. If you find yourself unusually frustrated or angry, ask yourself whether you have become overcommitted to achieving a goal that is your own but not your clients. Also look for ways to defuse any struggle you may have gotten into with them. Your task is to manage the process so that they can make their own decisions, based on their goals, while taking advantage of the expert information you can provide.

> *Case Example.* The father and the daughter in a family business decided that the time was right to globalize the company. The mother and two sons verbally agreed. As the planning advanced, mother and father began an old, familiar argument about investing the necessary money. The consultant helped the family see that this fight was helping to slow down the move into international markets. It was the family's way of saying that they had to take the time to plan carefully. The positive reframing of the owners' argument respected the resistance and encouraged the family to examine thoughtfully and at their own pace what the move meant for the company.

Guideline 7: Help the Family Business Members Understand and Improve Their Usual Pattern of Dealing with Change.

Set a tone that helps the family explore connections and patterns. Look past the current content and check out the process of past transitions. Ask questions that encourage learning. Who is most invested in this change? Who has the most to lose? And who is most upset that you are thinking of expanding the business? Are they usually the ones to be upset by change? What happened the last time the family decided to change the business?

Remember that people need information during a change in order to feel a certain amount of control. As a consultant to the process, however, you need to do more than ensure that information is disseminated. You need to attend to the power of information. Notice how people feel about information, how they share it, and how they use it to influence family relationships.

> *Case Example.* A couple calls you in as a financial adviser because their grown daughter wants to enter their business. You have an initial meeting with the couple, their son, age thirty-five, who is already in the business, and the daughter, age thirty-one. You learn that neither the family nor the business dealt effectively with the son's joining the firm nine years ago.
>
> At that time there had been many disagreements about finances and ownership. The employees did not know about the changes beforehand.

The parents and son avoided talking about job responsibilities and did not speak for two months, although they were "civil at work in order to get the job done." It took almost five years for them to get things straightened out at home and at work.

You explore both the content and the process of how the son entered the business. What did they learn from that experience? What do they want to avoid this time? Have they usually had a difficult time with change? What do they gain from generating a crisis? Do they thrive on chaos?

You help them to identify and articulate what bringing the daughter into the firm means to them and to learn more effective skills for dealing with change, resolving conflicts, and communicating with their employees. You also provide content expertise in business planning and resolving financial issues. You help them develop a mission statement for the business, reflecting the values and goals of both the family and the firm.

Conclusion

Content involves the concrete substance of consultation; process involves the patterns and relationships. Whenever a consultation in a content area seems to bog down or become stuck, try stepping back to look at the process. Attending to your own internal warning signals will enable you to do this more promptly and effectively. It will also let you know when to shift back to the content. If you find that the process issues are too complex or difficult for you to manage, it is wise to point this out to the family. Then work with them to find a consultant with process expertise, just as you would if they needed to find someone with special content expertise, such as tax planning.

Helping a family business requires a depth of knowledge and a wide variety of skills. Family business consultants come to this profession with markedly divergent training. The process-content framework is a tool that consultants can use effectively, whatever their profession of origin. It offers a useful alternative to the polarization traditionally emphasized in consultation models. By thoughtfully moving between process expertise and content expertise, you can be more effective in dealing with the unique demands of the family business.

References

Argyris, C. (1991). Teaching smart people how to learn. *Harvard Business Review*, 69 (3), 99–109.

Bateson, G., Jackson, D., Haley, J., & Weakland, J. (1968) A note on the double bind–1962. In D. Jackson (Ed.), *Communication, family and marriage, human communications, 1.* Palo Alto, CA: Science and Behavior Books, pp. 55–58.

Bork, D., Jaffe, D., Lane, S., & Heisler, G. (1993). *Consulting to family businesses: A guide for the attorney and other professionals.* Aspen, CO: Aspen Family Business Group.

Fisher, R., & Ury, W., with Patton, B. (Ed.). (1991). *Getting to yes: Negotiating agreement without giving in.* New York: Penguin Books.

Kanter, R. M. (1985). Managing the human side of change. *Management Review*, pp. 52–56.

Moore, C. (1986). *The mediation process: Practical strategies for resolving conflict.* San Francisco: Jossey-Bass.

Schaffer, R., & Thomson, H. (1992). Successful change programs begin with results. *Harvard Business Review*, 70 (1), 80–89.

Schein, E. (1988). *Process consultation: Its role in organizational development.* Reading, MA: Addison-Wesley.

Senge, P. (1991). *The fifth discipline: The art and practice of the learning organization.* New York: Doubleday.

Ury, W. (1993). *Getting past no: Negotiating your way from confrontations to cooperation.* New York: Bantam Books.

Watzlawick, P., Weakland, J., & Fisch, R. (1974). *Change: Principles of problem formation and problem resolution.* New York: Norton.

Whiteside, M., & Brown, F. (1991). Drawbacks of a dual systems approach to family firms: Can we expand our thinking? *Family Business Review*, 4 (4), 383–395.

Biographies

Jane Hilburt-Davis is principal at Key Resources, Lexington, Massachusetts, and is editor of the Case Series Project of the Family Firm Institute.

Peg Senturia is a family therapist and total quality management consultant, Brookline, Massachusetts.

ASSESSMENT TEST 5

It is now time to test your knowledge using the interactive assessment tool available online at www.familyenterprisebook.com/self-assessments. Enter "familyenterprise" as your password to proceed with the individual assessment. Your responses will be automatically scored and, in the event that you have entered an incorrect response, the correct answer will be provided.

1. Choose all responses that apply: Which of the following is a process skill?
   ☐ Ability to ask leading questions.
   ☐ Offering advice on an estate plan involving several businesses.
   ☐ Ability to share professional wisdom in a relevant and relatable manner.
   ☐ Ability to pick up on nonverbal cues.
   ☐ None of the above.

2. Choose all responses that apply: Which of the following is a content skill?
   ☐ Giving professional advice about a tax issue.
   ☐ Having the negotiation skills necessary to address the rules for dealing with a given issue.
   ☐ Suggesting ways to develop a board of advisors.
   ☐ Commenting on a decision regarding the sale of real estate.
   ☐ None of the above.

3. Choose all responses that apply: Which of the following is true of systems theory?
   ☐ Systems theory addresses a closed system only in which change is predictable and occurs in a linear fashion.
   ☐ Every event, according to systems theory, is interdependent with other events.
   ☐ General systems theory has its roots in fields like quantum physics and anthropology.
   ☐ The purpose of this type of thinking is to shift the focus from the enterprise to the individual.
   ☐ None of the above.

4. True or False: The advisor can avoid being triangled into a client system by giving good advice.

5. True or False: An example of a structure that maintains healthy boundaries is a family council.

6. True or False: Unclear roles and responsibilities are often a cause of problems in family enterprises.

7. True or False: Most interactions in family enterprises belong to closed systems.

8. True or False: Scapegoating is a way for a family in business to avoid discussing systemic issues.

9. True or False: Homeostasis is a term defining the boundaries of a family enterprise system.

10. True or False: The following comment is a process comment: "You both seem to agree on several items, in spite of the fact that you are angry with each other."

CHAPTER 6
Theoretical Frameworks in Family Enterprises

Three theoretical frameworks or models are particularly helpful for understanding family enterprise. They are: the three-circle model, the developmental model, and the balance point model.

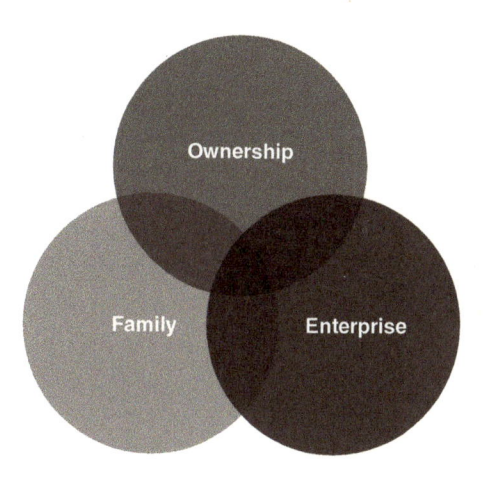

R. Tagiuri and John A. Davis, "The Three-Circle Model of Family Business," as referenced in "On the Goals of Successful Family Companies," *Family Business Review* 5, no. 1 (1992).

The *three-circle model* recognizes the systems of the three groups that are common to all family enterprises and is used to identify the various roles, responsibilities, and possible role conflicts of individuals.

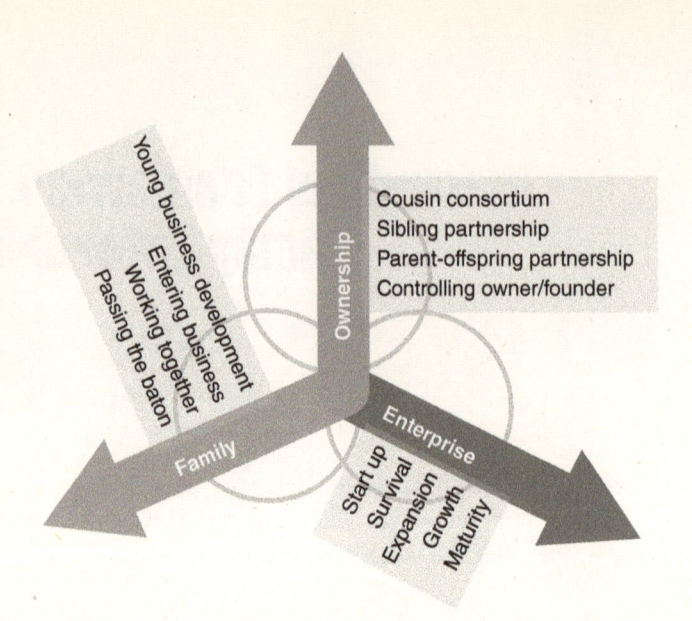

Ownership:
Cousin consortium
Sibling partnership
Parent-offspring partnership
Controlling owner/founder

Family:
Young business development
Entering business
Working together
Passing the baton

Enterprise:
Start up
Survival
Expansion
Growth
Maturity

Kelin Gersick, Ivan Lansberg, Michele Desjardins, and Barbara Dunn, adapted from "Stages and Transitions: Managing Change in the Family Business," *Family Business Review* 12, no. 4 (1999): 287–297.

The *developmental model* describes the developmental stages that the systems of family enterprises go through, the significance of their impact on the family enterprise system, and consultants' and advisors' work in and with them.

The *balance point model* is used to describe the alignment of family enterprise systems and identify the balance points within the enterprise. Establishing and maintaining alignment is key in this model, and an understanding of how to achieve this alignment is a useful skill for professionals.

KEY POINT

The three-circle model, the developmental model, and the balance point model are theoretical frameworks that are crucial to understanding family enterprises.

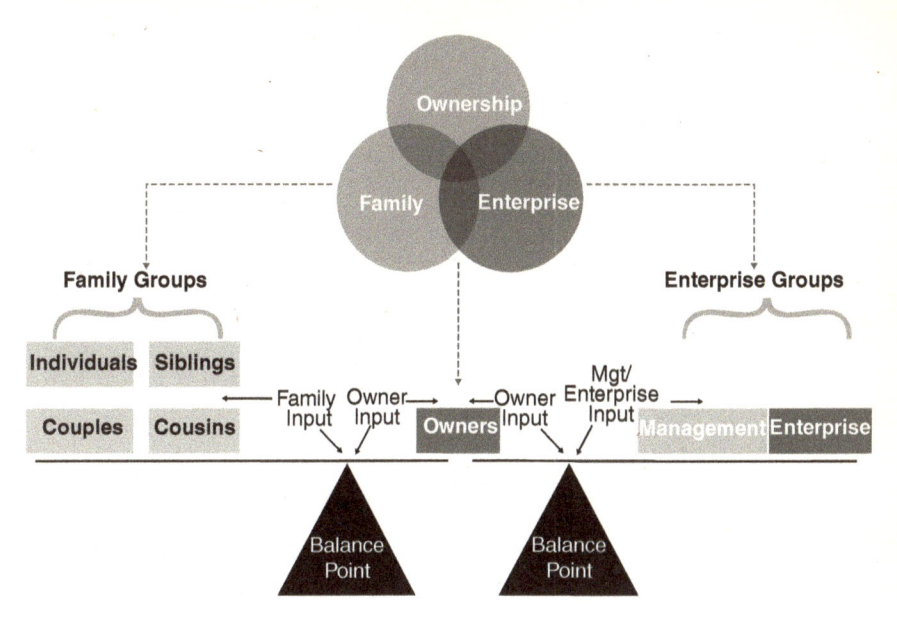

Theoretical Frameworks in Family Enterprises 83

© Larry Hause and Cary Tuteman. Adapted from presentation.

THE THREE-CIRCLE MODEL

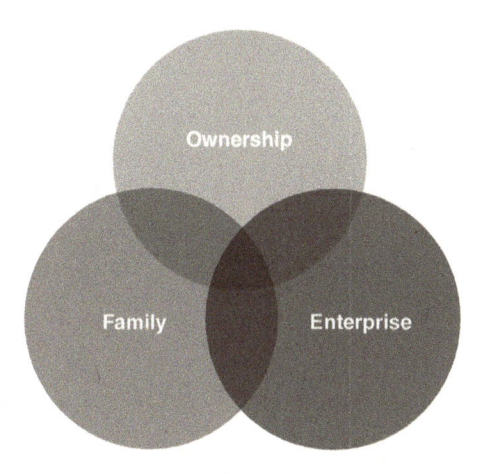

R. Tagiuri and John A. Davis, "The Three-Circle Model of Family Business," as referenced in "On the Goals of Successful Family Companies," *Family Business Review* 5, no. 1 (1992).

As its name suggests, the three-circle model understands family enterprises as comprised of three separate but overlapping and interdependent systems.

This model implies that there are systems within which decisions and interactions take place. Each system within the circle has its own functions, roles, and responsibilities.

Specifically:

- The enterprise system encompasses the enterprise operation, mission, strategies, managers, and other employees.
- The ownership system includes the enterprises' legal form, the distribution of ownership, and the goals and aspirations of those who own the business. In this model, this circle also includes the governance of the business.
- The family system involves the family (or families) connected to the enterprise. The family's goals, relationships, values, and communication patterns are all parts of the family system.

Each system within the circles is an open system, existing in the larger environment and interacting with each other.

Ownership/Governance System
Lawyers
Accountants
Estate Planners

Family Enterprise Consultants

Family System
Family Therapists

Enterprise System
Business/Organizational Development Consultants

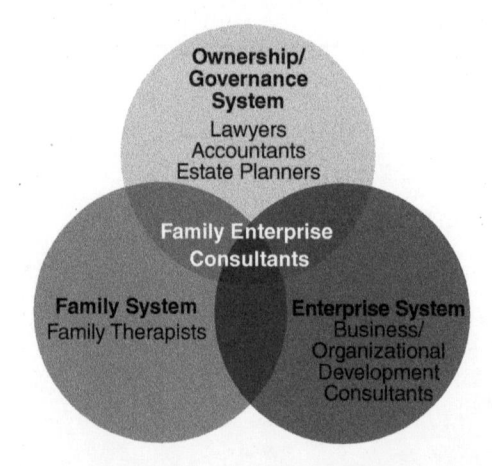

© Jane Hilburt-Davis and W. Gibb Dyer, Jr. (2003).

Each of the three groups or circles—the family, owners, and enterprise—has a system or systems (formal or informal) that are used to make decisions and guide interactions. It is important to remember that each system also has its own values, needs, goals, and responsibilities. In the three-circle model, the areas where the groups overlap indicate the areas that challenge the family enterprise.

When negotiating how each of these systems make decisions and interact, professionals working for family enterprises must always be aware of how their interactions in one circle will impact the other circles.

Additionally, what occurs in the other circles will impact what the professional is attempting to do with his or her clients.

In the family system, family members who are making decisions might put their focus on nurturing and educating or developing values.

In the owner/governance system, owners might make decisions and interact according to how they see the direction of the company being affected and how it impacts shareholder value.

And in the enterprise system, the ways in which decisions are made and interactions take place are often intended to carry out the direction as dictated by the owners and operations of the enterprise.

The Individuals Within the Systems

Because family members have various roles and differing interests, problems often emerge as the result of:

- Unclear roles and responsibilities.
- Conflicting roles and responsibilities.
- Unclear boundaries.
- Competing values, needs, and goals.
- Uncertainty over who has what authority.
- Uncertainty about who is accountable to whom.

External Stakeholders (Customers, Advisors, Suppliers)

Uncertainty about roles, responsibilities, authority, accountability, and competition arising from differing interests can result in behavior and outcomes that tend to be destructive or diffused. For example, making decisions in the business based on family reasons is bound to impact both negatively.

Clarity, acceptance, and alignment of those roles and responsibilities, however, can also be used constructively to harness energies to support the enterprise.

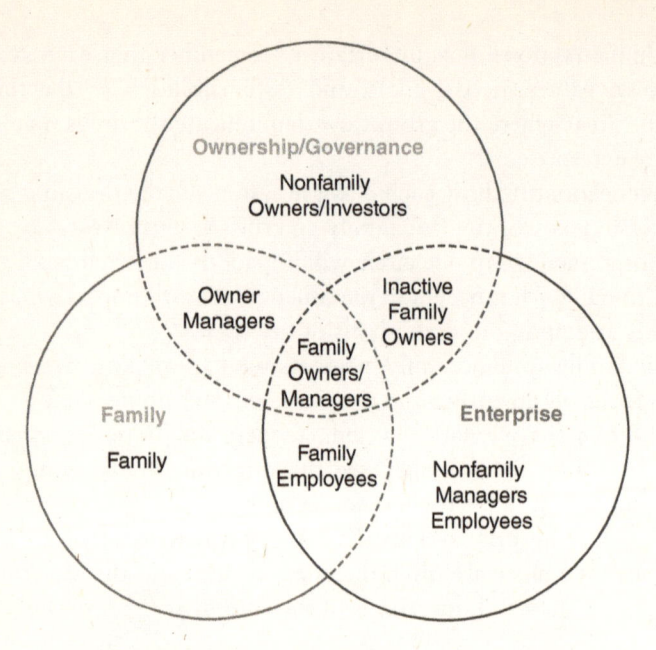

```
                    Ownership/Governance
                       Nonfamily
                    Owners/Investors

              Owner          Inactive
             Managers         Family
                      Family  Owners
                      Owners/
                      Managers
      Family                         Enterprise
                      Family
      Family         Employees      Nonfamily
                                    Managers
                                    Employees
```

External Stake Holders, e.g. customers, advisors, suppliers

Jane Hilburt-Davis and W. Gibb Dyer, Jr., *Consulting to Family Businesses* (San Francisco, CA: Jossey-Bass/Pfeiffer, 2003).

In every case, the individual is a key component of the family enterprise system because each of the primary groups is composed of individuals. Individuals in the family enterprise:

- Have ways by which they make decisions and interact with others.
- Have specific values, needs, and goals that motivate their behavior.
- Make decisions and/or do or do not take actions that affect other individuals.
- Perform functions and have responsibilities.

A family enterprise system contains many individuals, often of several generations and with distinctly different roles. Each individual also grows and changes over time, so the values, goals, and communication patterns change, thereby affecting the entire system. One of the challenges for advisors is to help the individuals find common ground.

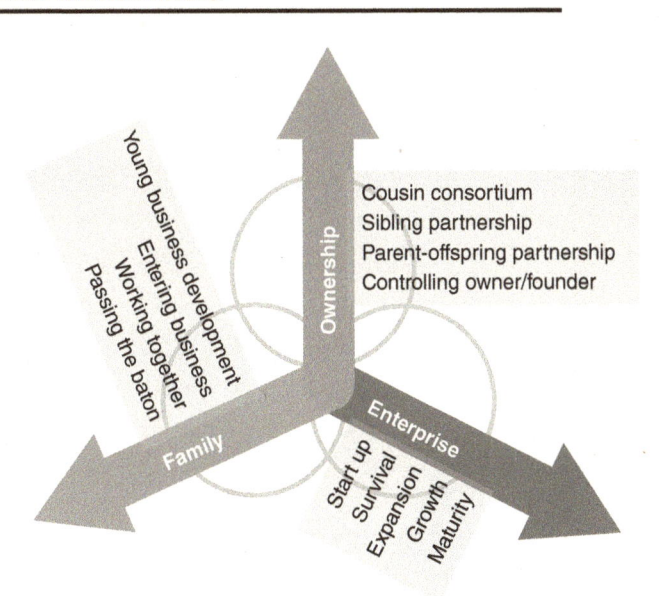

THE DEVELOPMENTAL MODEL

Ownership axis: Cousin consortium / Sibling partnership / Parent-offspring partnership / Controlling owner/founder

Family axis: Young business development / Entering business / Working together / Passing the baton

Enterprise axis: Start up / Survival / Expansion / Growth / Maturity

Kelin Gersick, Ivan Lansberg, Michele Desjardins, and Barbara Dunn, adapted from "Stages and Transitions: Managing Change in the Family Business," *Family Business Review* 12, no. 4 (1999): 287–297.

In the developmental model for enterprise ownership the controlling owner represents the stage where a single person or couple represents the senior management and ownership. Often this person is the founder or otherwise has the control or power to make the significant decisions regarding management and ownership.

Some have modified the original model by recognizing the parent-offspring partnership. Often this arrangement consists of a controlling owner who has transitioned ownership and/or management responsibilities to his/her children.

The sibling partnership represents the stage when ownership has passed to a succeeding generation consisting of siblings. At this stage the family enterprise has transitioned from the generation of the founder (the first generation) to the next succeeding generation (the second generation).

The cousin consortium represents the stage when family members hold ownership from different branches of the family (that is, cousins). Often this is when a family enterprise has transitioned from the second generation to the third generation.

THE BALANCE POINT MODEL

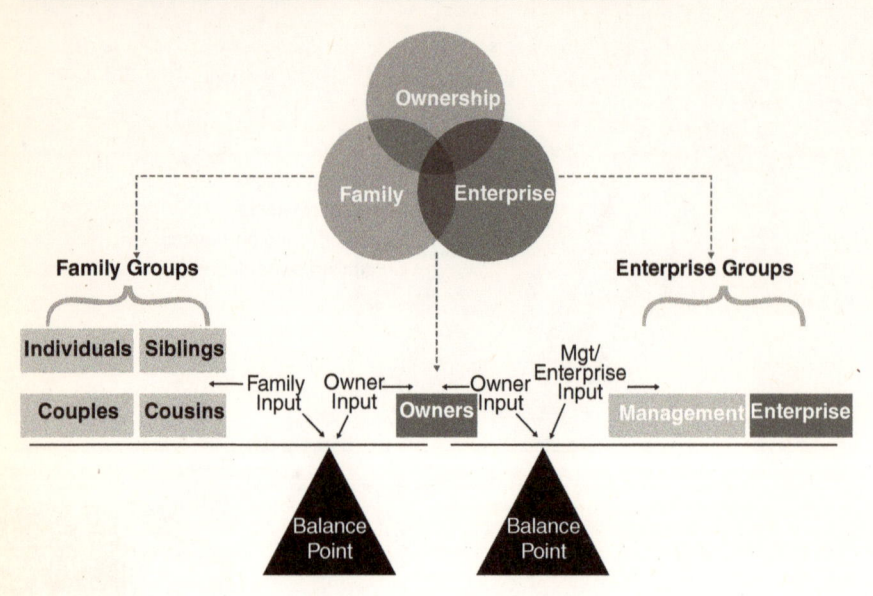

© Larry Hause and Cary Tuteman. Adapted from presentation.

The balance point model is defined as an alignment or integration of the family, owners, and enterprise interests—as well as a balance of separation and integration.

Separation can help clarify roles, responsibilities, authority, and accountability. Separation can also help identify values, needs, and goals.

Interdependence is needed to integrate or align the values, needs, and goals of individuals and groups. This interdependence can occur if there are effective "balancers" and "balance points" within the family enterprise.

The three groups are separate from each other for three reasons. First, each group has roles and responsibilities that are separate and distinct from the other groups. Second, each group has its own structure, policies, and procedures (system) to assist group members to make decisions and interact to carry out the group's responsibilities. Third, each group has its own values, needs, and goals.

In this model, to achieve the goal of balanced interdependence among the groups, the integration of the groups must be accomplished in a way that results in all of the interests being aligned or integrated. When this happens, the system is considered in balance.

Theoretical frameworks in family enterprise may take a number of forms. But in each case, the models must be able to accommodate and explain the complexity of family enterprise. Three models, in particular, are especially valuable. They are: the three-circle model, the developmental model, and the balance point model.

While the three-circle model focuses on the systems of the three groups common to all family enterprises and is typically used to identify the various roles, responsibilities, and possible role conflicts of individuals, the developmental model describes the developmental stages that the family enterprise systems go through. The developmental model also helps to illuminate the significance of those changes for the family enterprise system, as well as for the consultants' and advisors' work in and with that system.

The balance point model takes as its focal point the alignment of family enterprise systems as it seeks to identify the balance points within the enterprise. Establishing and maintaining alignment is crucial here, and an understanding of how to achieve this alignment is a useful skill for professionals.

Grasping and deploying these models is crucial to understanding and serving the needs of family enterprise. Indeed, family enterprises are at once interactive and dynamic, developmental, and in need of balance points.

ASSESSMENT TEST 6

It is now time to test your knowledge using the interactive assessment tool available online at www.familyenterprisebook.com/self-assessments. Enter "familyenterprise" as your password to proceed with the individual assessment. Your responses will be automatically scored and, in the event that you have entered an incorrect response, the correct answer will be provided.

1. Choose all responses that apply: What is meant by the enterprise balance point?
   □ The alignments of the owner's interests, needs, and values with those of the management.
   □ The alignment of the enterprise's interests, needs, and values with those of the management.
   □ The alignment of the family's interests, needs, and values with those of the management.
   □ None of the above.

2. Choose all responses that apply: Knowledge of family enterprise transitions is important because:
   ☐ The values, needs, and goals of each individual change over time and by events.
   ☐ Owners often resist developing a board of directors.
   ☐ Each stage of transition has its own challenges and tasks.
   ☐ None of the above.

3. Choose all responses that apply: Balancing, integrating, or aligning the interests of the owners and the enterprise/management requires:
   ☐ Understanding the interests of the owners.
   ☐ Understanding the interests of the managers.
   ☐ Evaluating whether the interests are the same or different.
   ☐ Seeing that the differences are reconciled, balanced, or aligned.
   ☐ None of the above.

4. Choose all responses that apply: In the development of an enterprise ownership:
   ☐ A sibling partnership often develops when the enterprise has transitioned into the second generation or the succeeding generation.
   ☐ The controlling owner often hands over senior management to an outside (nonfamily) party.
   ☐ The cousin consortium represents the stage when family members hold ownership from different branches of the family.
   ☐ Parents almost never pass on management responsibilities to their children.
   ☐ None of the above.

5. True or False: The cousin consortium stage is often filled with conflict.

6. True or False: The ideal family enterprise system would have each circle operating independently with no interactions among the circles.

7. True or False: A controlling ownership represents a stage with an owner who resists succession planning.

8. True or False: Balanced interdependence means that the values, needs, and goals of the various groups in the family enterprise are aligned.

9. True or False: An advisor can apply all three models when working with a family enterprise.

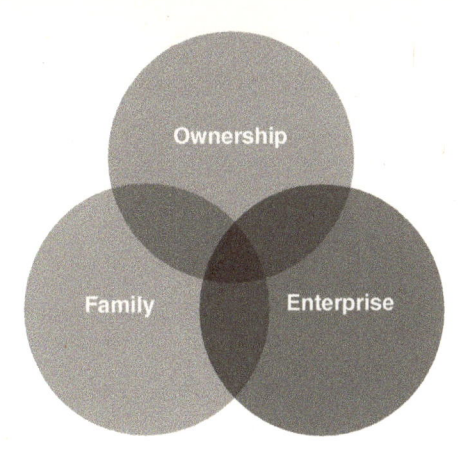

Theoretical Frameworks in Family Enterprises 91

R. Tagiuri and John A. Davis, "The Three-Circle Model of Family Business," as referenced in "On the Goals of Successful Family Companies," *Family Business Review* 5, no. 1 (1992).

10. Place the number of each of the roles below into the appropriate circle of the model on the diagram. (Keep the individual's and/or group's perspectives in mind.)

Roles

1. Nonfamily owner employee/manager

2. Owner, neither family nor employee

3. Family owner and employee

4. Family employee

5. Employee, neither family nor owner

6. Family, neither owner nor employee

7. Family owner

CHAPTER 7
Core Professions Working With Family Enterprises

Those working with family enterprises typically come from four core professions: legal, financial, management science, and behavioral science.

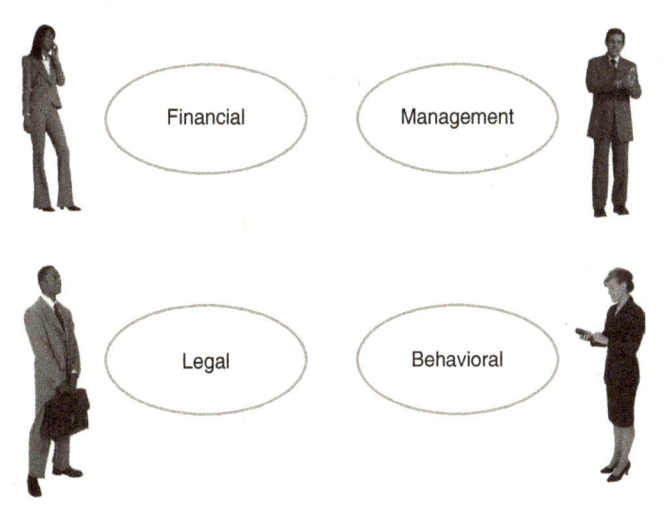

- Financial
- Management
- Legal
- Behavioral

This is not surprising, as family enterprises involve all of these professions at some point in time and in one way or another. Each of the four professions offers resources to help identify, assess, improve, and change various dimensions of family enterprises, including the way individuals make decisions and interact; the structures, policies, and procedures used by the family, owners, and enterprise systems to make decisions and interact; and the processes by which decisions are made and interactions occur to align the interests of the family, owners, and enterprise.

Legal professionals are employed by a family enterprise to structure the enterprise in compliance with laws and regulations, to establish and change agreements, to work with individuals in their estate and tax plans, and to deal with conflicts both within the enterprise and between the enterprise and outside entities.

As is well known, the legal system is society's way of creating and enforcing agreements and resolving disputes when individuals do not agree. The law allows individuals and groups to create an agreement or other legal arrangement to make legally enforceable all or parts of a family enterprise. Legal arrangements or agreements can be created in anticipation of an event, after an agreement, or following disputes.

Financial professionals are employed by a family enterprise for a variety of purposes. Such professionals aid in identifying, recording, and verifying financial data (this could include income, expenses, equity, assets, liabilities, and/or accounting). They also help to determine how much cash the owners and enterprise need and how to invest that cash (this might be in the form of financial planning or investment advisors).

Of course, financial professionals also assist in obtaining and maintaining access to cash (for example, banking, investment capital, and business brokers), thus ensuring that cash is available in the case of a catastrophic situation (such as death, natural disaster, or in the case of fraud insurance), or a planned liquidity event or transition.

Management science professionals can be employed to create, evaluate, and suggest changes to current structures or systems. They provide a range of services, such as:

- Organizational development
- Communication
- Business planning
- Management development
- Leadership evaluation and development
- Human resource development
- Strategic planning
- Compensation policies

Professionals from behavioral science typically facilitate making changes in an enterprise or with groups within the family business system. They are also trained to work with individuals. Services provided by behavioral science professionals include:

- Team building
- Interpersonal communication

- Addictions
- Individual or group therapy
- Executive coaching
- Leadership assessment and development
- Conflict management

> **KEY POINT**
>
> Almost all family enterprises work with legal, financial, management science, and behavioral science professionals at some point in their development.

DIFFERING PERCEPTUAL FILTERS

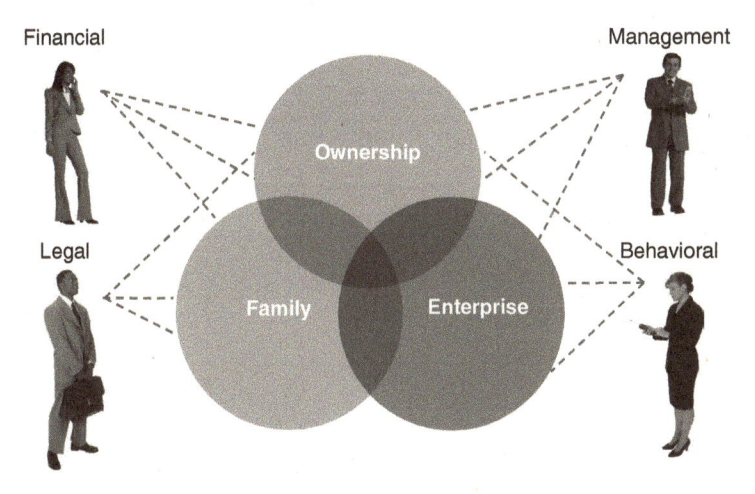

© Family Firm Institute.

Not surprisingly, how professionals from these core areas work with a family enterprise is often determined by their professional perceptions. For example, consider ways in which the four professions may deal with conflict. *Lawyers* may do so by creating or revising agreements, or through negotiation and litigation. *Financial advisors* might take a different approach by creating or revising financial or estate plans. Professionals from *management science* are more likely to recommend changes in decision-making procedures and compensation, and focus on team building. *Behavioral science* professionals initiate individual or group therapy, attempt to coach stakeholders to deal more effectively with elements of the enterprise system, and seek to develop effective communications strategies.

Yet despite these different, professionally determined perceptual filters, all four core professions deal with a number of recurring issues that cut across professional boundaries, including:

- Roles and boundaries within the family enterprise
- Intergenerational relationships
- Conflicts and disputes
- Visions and values
- Succession planning

UNDERSTAND THE DIFFERENCES AMONG THE CORE PROFESSIONS

There are two capacities in which those from the four core professions might apply their skills to family enterprises—as an advisor or as a consultant.

Family Enterprise Advisor: Entry Points

- Estate Planners / Accountants/Lawyers → Ownership/Governance System (Estate Planning)
- Family Therapists / Psychologists → Family System (Unity Planning)
- Business Consultants / OD Consultants → Enterprise Management & Leadership System (Succession Planning)

© Jane Hilburt–Davis. Adapted from Key Resources LLC.

Advisors are professionals who are primarily practicing their profession of origin when working with family enterprises. Indeed, the term *advisor* is meant to include those professionals who view themselves as family enterprise advisors as opposed to family enterprise consultants.

Both the family enterprise advisor and the family wealth advisor have one or more specific areas of expertise. For instance, a family enterprise advisor and/or a family wealth advisor could be an estate planner, tax accountant, family therapist, or an executive coach.

Consultants are professionals who have further training beyond their profession of origin. The consultant's role is often to work in the center of the three-circle model at the interface of the family, enterprise, and ownership.

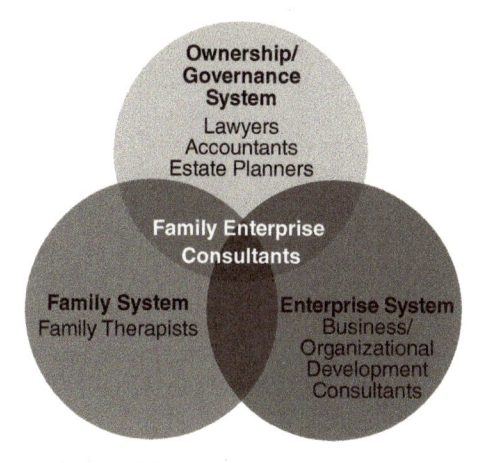

Ownership/Governance System
Lawyers
Accountants
Estate Planners

Family Enterprise Consultants

Family System
Family Therapists

Enterprise System
Business/Organizational Development Consultants

Jane Hilburt–Davis and W. Gibb Dyer, Jr., *Consulting to Family Businesses* (San Francisco, CA: Jossey–Bass/Pfeiffer, 2003).

Family enterprise consultants tend mainly to have a process focus and are there to help integrate and facilitate the plans and interactions of the family, ownership, and management systems as well as the individuals within these systems. Unlike the advisors, they typically no longer practice in their profession of origin, although they are usually experts in one of the core professions and have done further training.

The consultant helps to integrate plans and to improve interaction between the groups and the individuals and works with both process and content, with emphasis on process in the change effort.

As noted above, the consultant's role is often to work in the center of the three-circle model and assist clients in ensuring both that individuals within each group are working effectively within the group, and that the groups are working effectively together. In this mode, the three circles include family, enterprise, and ownership. Each circle represents the overlapping systems of the family enterprise. What distinguishes family enterprise consultants is their work at the boundaries where these three systems overlap.

In addition to the advisor and the consultant, there is another person to whom the client will often turn first for advice—the trusted advisor. This person has a special personal relationship with the client. The trusted advisor's role is to provide a perspective on any topic that the client raises. He or she is not necessarily from one of the core professions and may change over time or in various circumstances. The trusted advisor can even change during a single engagement. One person might be a trusted advisor for some purposes, and another person might be a trusted advisor for another purpose, and multiple people in the system may mean multiple trusted advisors.

In fact, the trusted advisor may not be a professional at all. The "2007 American Family Business Survey," sponsored by MassMutual, Kennesaw State University, and the Family Firm Institute, noted that the client's most-trusted advisor changed between 2002 and 2007. When considering the top three most-trusted advisors, business owners ranked their accountant first, just as they did in 2002; spouses second, up from fifth in 2002; and their lawyer third, down from second in 2002.

The trusted advisor, however, can be from any one of the core professions (legal, financial, management, or behavioral science) and may or may not be officially providing services to the client.

The point is to recognize that clients often have a trusted advisor to whom they turn for advice. For instance, the client might turn to the trusted advisor for his/her opinion on whether the client should do what an outside professional recommends. It can help the professional to include the trusted advisor as much as possible in the process so that the trusted advisor is in a position to respond when the client seeks his/her advice.

KEY POINT

In addition to the advisor and the consultant, family enterprises may have a trusted advisor.

Core Professions Working With Family Enterprises

ASSESSMENT TEST 7

It is now time to test your knowledge using the interactive assessment tool available online at www.familyenterprisebook.com/self-assessments. Enter "familyenterprise" as your password to proceed with the individual assessment. Your responses will be automatically scored and, in the event that you have entered an incorrect response, the correct answer will be provided.

1. Choose all responses that apply: Which of the following belong to the core disciplines of professionals who advise family enterprises?
   ☐ Legal.
   ☐ Financial.
   ☐ Government.
   ☐ Management science.
   ☐ Behavioral science.
   ☐ Vendors.
   ☐ None of the above.

2. Choose all responses that apply: An accountant hired by the founder and owner will find that her ability to accomplish the work can be impacted by the following people (even if they don't work in the business):
   ☐ Sister-in-law.
   ☐ Oldest brother.
   ☐ Father.
   ☐ None of the above.

3. Choose all responses that apply: A consultant deploying the three-circle model should assess:
   ☐ Whether each of the groups (family, owners, enterprise) is working effectively and whether all three work together effectively.
   ☐ What the goals are of each of the groups in the consultation.
   ☐ Whether there are outstanding issues that need to be resolved before the enterprise can make gains.
   ☐ None of the above.

4. True or False: Intergenerational relationships are an issue that professionals from all the core disciplines might address.

5. True or False: The main difference between advisors and consultants is the number of years of experience.

6. True or False: A family enterprise experiencing problems developing a succession plan only needs an advisor from the legal profession.

7. True or False: The trusted advisor is never a family member.

8. True or False: Recurring issues that professionals confront in the context of working with family enterprise clients typically include conflicts, succession planning, and intergenerational relationships.

9. True or False: Family enterprise advisors operate from the center of the three-circle model.

10. True or False: Accountants are most likely to enter family enterprise through the ownership/governance system.

CHAPTER 8
Multidisciplinary Professional Teams

Family businesses are increasingly demanding that their advisors work as a team. Multidisciplinary teamwork is not unique to family business advising. Hospitals, schools, and organizations of all sizes appreciate the value of developing teams of individuals with accountability to separate departments and an allegiance to the larger company or organization, sometimes referred to as cross-functional teams.

Professionals advising family businesses also understand that working together in a team benefits the client. Thus an increasing number of groups are offering multidisciplinary services. Those who want to work independently will often find that the complexity of the client's problems is simply too challenging to be adequately addressed from one discipline.

In order to gain the potential benefits of a team approach, the professionals involved must understand what each brings and how best to work together.

TYPES OF TEAMS

There are several models of teams. All teams function on a continuum in terms of how often they work together, the level of coordination and organization of the team, and the members' commitment to each other.

Teams may be categorized as follows:

- A consulting firm (typically interdisciplinary) is a pre-existing team that is hired by the client.
- A collaborative (multidisciplinary) team is one in which advisors from different disciplines meet in a study group forum, get to know each other's work, and bring each other into client situations on an as-needed basis or use in a shadow consulting function.

- An accidental team is one in which advisors meet and connect through the client only, with minimal coordination.
- A dysfunctional team is one in which advisors are unknown to one another, even if they are working with the same client, and work with minimal to no coordination.

CHALLENGES TEAMS FACE

Despite their growing acceptance in the field, and the recognition that teaming the advisors leads to better and more cost-effective advice, the multidisciplinary team still poses several challenges.

Indeed, some combination of the following questions typically emerge:

- Will there be or who will be the quarterback?
- Who will see that work gets coordinated?
- How will the billing be handled?
- How will differences be managed?
- Who will be the liaison to the client?
- How will the client be sold on the multidisciplinary team?
- How will we deal with competition for the best idea, suggestions, and recommendations?
- How will everyone find the time necessary to plan and best meet the client's needs?

Beyond such questions, perspectives and skills brought to a team can vary widely. And that in turn can affect the relationships that each of the professionals has with clients, especially at the level of:

- Boundaries
- Process/content
- Indirect/direct interventions

Behavioral	Management	Financial/Legal

Therapy ⟷ Counseling ⟷ Coaching ⟷ Facilitation ⟷ Consultancy ⟷ Advice

PROCESS .... CONTENT

© The Family Firm Institute, Inc.

Therapists, for example, have clear boundaries with their clients. They would not typically have lunch or play golf with them, whereas accountants on the other end of the continuum often have close personal relationships with clients.

At the therapy end of the continuum, the work is done almost exclusively with process. By contrast, at the other end of the spectrum are law and finance, where the work is done with the emphasis on content.

In terms of interventions, things vary as well. At the therapy end, most of the interventions are indirect, whereas at the other end of the advising spectrum, the interventions are direct and involve the explicit giving of advice.

Of course, family enterprises want several things from their advisors. They want comprehensive advice, specific products and services, breadth and depth of knowledge, openness and knowledge of the "soft side," and multidisciplinary teams with someone to coordinate and integrate advice. Hence it follows that achieving balance is crucial to working with family enterprises.

KEY POINT

To maximize the potential benefits of a multidisciplinary team approach to working with family enterprises, individuals must be aware of their own profession and consider how to best work together with individuals from other disciplines.

You have now finished Chapter 8. Before doing the assessments, please read the following, "The Effects of Goal Orientation and Client Feedback on the Adaptive Behaviors of Family Enterprise Advisors" from *Family Business Review*.

The Effects of Goal Orientation and Client Feedback on the Adaptive Behaviors of Family Enterprise Advisors

Walter D. Davis, University of Mississippi, Oxford, MS, USA
Clay Dibrell, University of Mississippi, Oxford, MS, USA
Justin B. Craig, Northeastern University, Boston, MA, USA
Judy Green, Family Firm Institute, Boston, MA, USA
Corresponding Author: Clay Dibrell, University of Mississippi

Abstract

Family enterprise advisors work on complex and unique problems for their family enterprise clients. Little attention has been given to these professionals and their abilities to provide innovative solutions. In this study, our aim is to understand more about family enterprise advisors (N = 231). To achieve this objective, we hypothesize that the effects of advisor goal orientation (i.e., learning orientation, proving orientation, and avoidance orientation) on adaptive behaviors (i.e., personal bricolage and individual innovative behavior) are mediated by the quality of feedback received from clients. The results indicate that quality of feedback partially mediates the relationships between goal orientation and these behaviors. We conclude by providing a practitioner model explaining how advisors may adapt to different family enterprise client role environments.

Keywords

family enterprise advisors, goal orientation, feedback quality, personal bricolage, individual innovative behavior

Family enterprises are different from other businesses. Likewise, advisors and consultants who serve family enterprises face challenges that are distinct from those faced by other advisors and consultants. Though it is widely accepted that advisors play a crucial role within family enterprises (for an excellent overview, see Strike, 2012), there is a dearth of academic research that focuses on the behavior and functioning of this group of stakeholders. This is curious given the valuable contributions advisors and consultants make to the sustainability of the vast family enterprise sector in countries across the globe. We address this shortcoming using survey data gathered from members of the Family Firm Institute (FFI). In particular, we are interested in understanding how FFI member advisors[1] who work with family enterprises in a "formal" (rather than informal) capacity (Strike, 2012) are able to adapt to the needs of these unique clients through the creative orchestration of personal resources (i.e., personal bricolage) and through the development of innovative responses (i.e., individual innovative behavior).

The roles played by advisors to family firms are complex and fluid for several reasons. First, the complex interaction of family, ownership, and management systems needs to be assessed, interpreted, and responded to appropriately (J. M. Goodman, 1998; Mitchell, Morse, & Sharma, 2003; Strike, 2012; Tagiuri & Davis, 1996). Second, the multigenerational involvement in some if not all of these systems adds an additional layer of complexity not found in other contexts (Bammens, Voordeckers, & van Gils, 2008; Upton, Vinton, Seaman, & Moore, 1993). Third, there is often an omnipresent founder, some who have long passed, whose powerful influence over the family and the business needs to be understood (P. S. Davis & Harveston, 1999; Jaffe & Lane, 2004). Fourth, a culture of privacy and a tradition of secrecy within the family create barriers to trust that are difficult to penetrate in the short run and require higher levels of social skill in the long run as advisors engage with multiple stakeholders (Lester & Cannella, 2006; Levinson, 1983; Strike, 2012).

For these reasons, creative uses of resources and personal innovative behaviors are likely to be very important for successful performance among family firm advisors. This group operates within a distinctively different client context, as indicated in a preponderance of the family business literature (see Chua, Chrisman, & Sharma, 1999; Strike, 2012).

Because of the intricate and varying role environment faced by these advisors, a "have-solution-will-travel" consulting model will often be inappropriate for servicing the needs of their clients (Levinson, 1983). That is, because of the additional complexity introduced by the family system, each assignment has the potential to be vastly different and nuanced. Given the multifaceted role environment these advisors face, their assignment is likely to be changing and ambiguous, even more so than it would be in "mainstream" client–consultancy relationships. Accordingly, we suggest that the need for adaptation and innovation is greater in these environments than in traditional work settings and in traditional advisor–management relations.

Despite the acceptance that family firm advisors operate in a uniquely dynamic environment, there has been little research to determine how they manage this environment. In this article, we argue that family enterprise advising and consulting professionals need to generate high-quality feedback from clients and then use feedback as a resource for personal adaptability and innovation. Feedback is vital to any advisor–client relationship. Given the complicated nature (e.g., because of the concurrent interaction of family systems and business systems) of their family enterprise clients, advisors are likely to work in feedback environments that are more intricate and/or vague than in traditional job settings where feedback is provided by either supervisors or formal organizational reporting systems. We propose the success with which they generate feedback will affect how well they creatively combine and recombine resources, and the extent to which they are able to innovate their own roles.

To further enrich our understanding of how family enterprise advisors adapt to their complex role environment, we look to individual differences in goal orientation that have the potential to explain how diverse advisors take differing approaches to their work.

Comprising three relatively stable dimensions (i.e., learning orientation, proving orientation, and avoidance orientation), goal orientation is an established construct that distinguishes how individuals develop or demonstrate ability in achievement settings (DeShon & Gillespie, 2005; VandeWalle & Cummings, 1997).

Our research question, therefore, can be stated in two parts:

In the context of family enterprise advisors, (a) how do individual predispositions toward goal accomplishment (goal orientation) affect the acquisition of quality feedback from clients and (b) how does this in turn affect adaptive behaviors such as personal bricolage and individual innovative behavior?

Our motivation in this research is not to compare the community of family enterprise advisors with other advisors. Rather, we intend to use the constructs of goal orientation, feedback environment, personal bricolage, and individual innovative behavior to appreciate how family enterprise advisors function.

The article proceeds as follows: We explain how personal bricolage and individual innovative behavior are adaptive behaviors useful for coping with complicated role environments. We then describe the importance of feedback as a valuable resource that advisors often seek in environments that require adaptation. We link advisor goal orientation to the acquisition of quality feedback from clients and hypothesize that quality feedback mediates the relationships between the three dimensions of advisor goal orientation (learning, proving, and avoidance) and advisor adaptive behaviors (personal bricolage and individual innovative behavior). Next, we report our empirical examination of how individual differences in goal orientation affect the acquisition of quality feedback from clients, and subsequent advisor adaptive behaviors (personal bricolage and individual innovative behavior), as depicted in Figure 8.1. Finally, we conclude with a discussion of our results and avenues for further research.

Literature Review and Hypothesis Development

To answer our research questions, we draw from broader theoretical perspectives used by scholars to study how individuals proactively manage their own work roles.

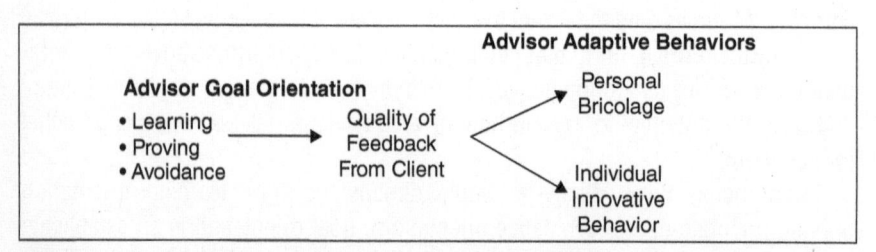

FIGURE 8.1 The Impact of Goal Orientation of Family Enterprise Advisors on Client Feedback and Advisor Adaptive Behaviors

For instance, recent perspectives on work design emphasize that individuals can be proactive in defining the nature and boundaries of their work roles (Grant & Parker, 2009). In many work settings, individuals are required to adapt to rapidly changing role requirements. Accordingly, research on individual performance has evolved such that researchers are interested in not only task performance but also how individuals self-manage, creatively use, reconfigure, and recombine available personal role management.

A separate but related stream of literature asserts individuals can proactively manage the feedback environment (Ashford, Blatt, & VandeWalle, 2003; Ashford & Cummings, 1983). From this viewpoint, feedback is not something that is simply provided by supervisors and organizational reporting systems. Rather, individuals make conscious decisions about which feedback resources are needed and proactively monitor and/or seek feedback from others. Advisors to family enterprises work in environments that encourage, and likely require, them to manage their own feedback environment and to innovate their personal work roles.

Personal Bricolage, Individual Innovative Behavior, and the Role of Feedback

Personal bricolage involves creatively combining and recombining existing resources for the purpose of goal accomplishment. More specifically, Baker and Nelson (2005) define bricolage as "making do by applying combinations of the resources at hand to new problems and opportunities" (p. 334). These authors identify three primary elements of bricolage. First, bricolage represents a bias toward action and active engagement with problems or opportunities. Pivotal to bricolage is a willingness to experiment with new ways to accomplish goals without worrying about whether they have the "right" tools, resources, or skills at hand. Put simply, bricolage involves trying to find ways of addressing new challenges. A second element of bricolage is a reliance on "the resources at hand," which includes resources already controlled and those that are freely or cheaply available. Finally, bricolage involves "the combination of resources for new purposes," which is more than simply conserving resources for their original purposes. Rather, it involves the creative recombination of resources toward purposes for which they were not originally intended (Hmieleski & Corbett, 2006; Senyard, Baker, & Davidsson, in press).

Individual innovative behavior occurs when individuals purposefully introduce and implement new ideas, procedures, products, or processes in the workplace (Yuan & Woodman, 2010). Innovation has similarities with creative behavior in that it involves the creation of new ideas. However, it is distinct in that it also involves the *implementation* of new ideas. Implementation may require a number of related behaviors, such as acquiring resources, applying new work methods, altering work routines, or persuading other actors within an organization to alter their behaviors (Scott & Bruce, 1994; Yuan & Woodman, 2010). In our study, we investigate the role that feedback plays as a personal resource useful for adaptation and the role that personal goal orientation (i.e., learning, proving, avoidance; Brett & VandeWalle, 1999) plays in the acquisition of the feedback resource. We argue that high-quality feedback from clients is a personal resource that advisors can use for personal bricolage and individual innovative behavior.

Feedback quality is the extent to which feedback provides information to its recipient that is helpful for (a) understanding how well one is doing one's work and (b) improving performance.

Feedback in work settings is vital to optimum performance. As such, the feedback environment in which work is conducted can be one of the most powerful factors affecting how individuals react to performance situations (Cusella, 1987). In the context of our research, quality feedback can be a useful personal resource for advisors for several reasons. First, feedback signaling a gap between current performance and performance goals can lead to greater motivation and more focused efforts to achieve goals (Locke & Latham, 1990). Second, it provides information useful for correcting inappropriate task strategies (Ilgen, Fisher, & Taylor, 1979), especially when it is more specific (W. D. Davis, Carson, Ammeter, & Treadway, 2005; J. S. Goodman, Wood, & Hendrickx, 2004) and of higher quality (Steelman, Levy, & Snell, 2004). Third, feedback reduces uncertainty about how well (or poorly) one is performing (Ashford, 1986; Ashford & Cummings, 1983). Because uncertainty can often distract individuals from performing their duties (Kanfer & Ackerman, 1989), quality feedback that reduces uncertainty can lead to more efficient strategies for accomplishing goals (Kanfer & Ackerman, 1989).

Given that feedback is an important personal resource for accomplishing work-related tasks and for fulfilling work role expectations, individuals are often motivated to seek feedback (Ashford, 1986; Ashford et al., 2003). Individuals are proactive managers of their feedback environment and can seek or generate their own feedback when it is not provided by some external source (Ashford & Cummings, 1983). In other words, individuals do not just passively wait to receive feedback from their environment, but rather they proactively pursue performance-related information. Feedback seeking can be accomplished by simply observing the reactions of others or by actively inquiring from others (Ashford, 1986). The quality of feedback is becoming increasingly important, as many work environments lack immediate and specific feedback while requiring individuals to rely on their own judgment to determine the requirements of the job and how these requirements can be fulfilled (Neck & Manz, 1996). We argue that feedback plays a significant role in the adaptive behaviors of family firm advisors.

Goal Orientation, Feedback Quality, and Adaptive Behavior

Goal orientation comprises three dimensions: *learning* orientation, *proving* orientation, and *avoidance* orientation. These are relatively stable predispositions toward developing or demonstrating one's own ability in achievement settings (DeShon & Gillespie, 2005; VandeWalle & Cummings, 1997).

Learning orientation arises from a belief that increased effort can lead to learning, increased ability, and better performance (Dweck, 1986; VandeWalle, Cron, & Slocum, 2001). Persons high in learning orientation are motivated to learn new competencies in a task, and focus their attention on the refinement of existing skills or the development of new skills (Brett & VandeWalle, 1999). In work environments that require a great deal of self-management, learning orientation is often a strong predictor of performance (Fisher & Ford, 1998; Porath & Bateman, 2006; Seijts, Latham, Tasa, & Latham, 2004). Importantly, the positive impact of learning orientation on performance is likely because of (a) its effect on feedback seeking and (b) its effect on task strategies.

Persons high in learning orientation place a high value on feedback and are more proactive feedback seekers (VandeWalle & Cummings, 1997; VandeWalle et al., 2001). They engage in feedback seeking because they see feedback as useful for developing skills and improving performance (VandeWalle & Cummings, 1997; VandeWalle et al., 2001). They not only seek out more information but also are more likely to seek the type of feedback information that will help them develop new skills. On receiving feedback, these individuals are likely to stay focused on task learning rather than focused on their own performance relative to others (VandeWalle et al., 2001). There is also evidence that persons high in learning orientation are actually less dependent on the provision of feedback from external sources such as supervisors, coworkers, or formal feedback systems (W. D. Davis et al., 2005). They are likely to be better able to generate their own feedback and take a more proactive approach in acquiring feedback that is actually useful to them as a resource, which subsequently can be used for adaptation. Thus, we expect that even when there is little feedback available from others, family firm advisors with high learning orientation are better able to compensate for this by generating their own insight and will ultimately have higher quality feedback available to them.

Family businesses provide additional challenges to section of family, ownership, and the business (Strike, 2012; Tagiuri & Davis, 1996). Given the close association of the family with the firm built over many years, even decades, family members have strong deep-rooted perspectives, which manifest in emotional commitment and the use of a distinctive communication medium (Aldrich & Cliff, 2003; Arregle, Hitt, Sirmon, & Very, 2007). This form of social bonding is distinctive to each family and is a key contributor to the development of unwritten, but shared, understanding among actors (Danes, 2011). As much of the knowledge is protected by the family, and is intentionally difficult to access, we suggest that family enterprise advisors will often find it more difficult to acquire high-quality feedback from their clients (Strike, 2012) and will need to be more proactive in their approach to gathering feedback. Advisors high in learning orientation will distinguish themselves in their willingness to proactively learn the unique nuances of the family enterprise client context by acquiring high-quality feedback.

Hypothesis 1: For family enterprise advisors, learning orientation is positively related to feedback quality.

Learning orientation also affects the approach that individuals take toward improving work performance. Persons high in learning orientation are more likely to observe and analyze their own task strategies and to experiment with alternative ways in order to improve these task strategies (Steele-Johnson, Beauregard, Hoover, & Schmidt, 2000). In situations where the development of new skills is necessary to improve work performance, learning-oriented individuals engage in more "elaboration" of task strategies (Fisher & Ford, 1998; Steele-Johnson et al., 2000). Elaboration is an effort to develop new schemas for accomplishing work. New schemas are developed by experimenting with new ways of doing things. This elaboration or experimentation leads to the development of new task strategies and learning from failures in an attempt to adjust task strategies. In the long run, elaboration explains why persons high in learning orientation often perform better in learning and training settings (Fisher & Ford, 1998).

Family business advisors function in complex role environments, which have their origins in relationship conflicts among members of the owning family (Eddleston & Kellermanns, 2007). In such complex role environments, learning orientation is likely to lead to more innovation of one's work role, as well as more creative use of existing resources (i.e., personal bricolage). Evidence to support this is presented in a study by Hirst, Van Knippenberg, and Zhou (2009), which found that learning orientation was positively related to creativity. We propose that quality feedback also plays an important role in the processes of personal bricolage and individual innovative behavior. In other words, persons high in learning orientation are better able to engage in personal bricolage and individual innovative behavior because they acquire higher quality feedback. Accordingly, we propose that the effect of learning orientation on personal bricolage and individual innovative behavior is mediated by the quality of feedback family advisors receive from their clients.

Hypothesis 2: For family enterprise advisors, learning orientation is positively related to (a) personal bricolage and (b) individual innovative behavior.

Hypothesis 3: For family enterprise advisors, the effect of learning orientation on (a) personal bricolage and (b) individual innovative behavior is mediated by feedback quality.

Research indicates that advisors often choose different approaches to managing their relationships with clients (e.g., Strike, 2012). For example, some family advisors attempt to avoid interpersonal relationships with the family in order to not become entangled in family dynamics, such as being an intermediary among conflicting members of the family (White, 2007). This may enable the family advisors to focus more on completing the business-related assignment than having their efforts distracted by family members competing for their time. In our study, we argue that personality traits, such as proving and avoidance orientation, may play a role in determining advisors' decisions about how they engage with family enterprise clients, especially with respect to the feedback they acquire from clients.

Proving orientation and *avoidance* orientation arise from a personal belief that personal ability is unlikely to change because it is relatively stable and perhaps even innate. Thus, personal ability is difficult to develop via learning new task strategies or through increased effort (Dweck & Leggett, 1988; Elliot & Harackiewicz; 1996; VandeWalle et al., 2001). Persons high in *proving* orientation attempt to demonstrate task competence and gain favorable judgments from others (VandeWalle, 1997). Persons high in *avoidance* orientation seek to avoid the demonstration of low ability and the unfavorable judgments that might arise from poor performance. These attributes of proving and avoidance orientation are likely to affect how advisors acquire feedback from clients.

Because persons high in proving and avoidance orientations tend to believe that performance is based on innate ability, they often view feedback as simply an evaluation of that innate ability. They are interested in feedback that tells them how well they are performing relative to others (i.e., outcome feedback) rather than feedback that tells them how to improve their performance (i.e., process feedback). Accordingly, these individuals may be more self-focused than task-focused following feedback—concerned more with how they perform relative to others than with using the feedback as a resource for performance improvement (Kluger & DeNisi, 1996; VandeWalle et al., 2001). We would not expect them to acquire the type of high-quality feedback needed for personal bricolage or individual innovative behavior. Thus, we anticipate family advisors who have a proving or avoidance orientation will be less likely to seek out feedback from their family enterprise clients.

Hypothesis 4: For family enterprise advisors, proving orientation is negatively related to feedback quality.

Hypothesis 5: For family enterprise advisors, avoidance orientation is negatively related to feedback quality.

Proving and avoidance orientations also affect the approach individuals take to performance improvement. Proving and avoidance orientations often lead to "rehearsal" of task strategies rather than elaboration of task strategies (Fisher & Ford, 1998; Steele-Johnson et al., 2000). Rehearsal simply involves practicing an existing task strategy rather than trying to learn new task strategies. Rehearsal is a simpler learning strategy that involves less cognitive effort. It is unlikely to lead to the learning of new procedural knowledge. As persons high in performance orientation view high effort as a reflection of low ability, they will use rehearsal strategies to minimize effort (Fisher & Ford, 1998). If the existing task strategy is appropriate, then rehearsal will likely lead to performance improvement over time. On the other hand, if the existing task strategy is incorrect or needs refinement, then rehearsal will simply reinforce an inappropriate approach to task accomplishment.

When work strategies need adjustment, elaboration is required to gain new procedural knowledge. In complex role environments, which are the purview of family business advisors (Strike, 2012), persons high in proving orientation or avoidance orientation are less likely to engage in innovation and less likely to creatively use or recombine resources. Furthermore, expected image risks associated with innovative behavior are likely to lead to lower personal innovation (Yuan & Woodman, 2010). As persons high in avoidance or proving orientation tend to be more concerned with personal image, it seems likely that they would perceive innovative behavior as more risky, and would in turn be less likely to engage in such behavior. Advisors high in avoidance or proving orientation may be concerned about the impact of failure on their professional reputation. Nicholson, Shepherd, and Woods (2010) discovered that professional reputation was one of the key attributes considered by families when hiring a family enterprise advisor. Adaptive behaviors such as bricolage and innovation carry greater risks, as they may lead to failure, resulting in a diminished professional reputation. To avoid these risks, family enterprise advisors who are high on either proving or avoidance orientation may be more likely to implement existing approaches to solving a client's problem rather than engaging in new and more effective approaches. Furthermore, these advisors may also be reluctant to seek feedback for fear of injuring their professional reputation. Accordingly, we expect advisors high in proving or avoidance orientation will be less likely to acquire feedback for the purposes of bricolage or innovative behavior:

Hypothesis 6: For family enterprise advisors, proving orientation is negatively related to (a) personal bricolage and (b) individual innovative behavior.

Hypothesis 7: For family enterprise advisors, the effect of proving orientation on (a) personal bricolage and (b) individual innovative behavior is mediated by feedback quality.

Hypothesis 8: For family enterprise advisors, avoidance orientation is negatively related to (a) personal bricolage and (b) individual innovative behavior.

Hypothesis 9: For family enterprise advisors, the effect of avoidance orientation on (a) personal bricolage and (b) individual innovative behavior is mediated by feedback quality.

Method

Sample

Data were collected through an online questionnaire following the procedures articulated by Dillman, Smyth, and Christian (2009). In association with the FFI, we drew on a potential sample of 1,700 FFI members. According to the FFI website, "The Family Firm Institute is the leading membership association worldwide for professionals serving the family enterprise field. It provides a global forum for practitioners, academics and others to acquire multidisciplinary knowledge while engaging in collaborative opportunities." Invitations to participate in the study were disseminated to members via a weekly newsletter and personalized e-mail. Of the approximately 1,700 invitations delivered, we received 314 mostly completed responses, for a response rate of approximately 18.5%. Testing for the effects associated with nonresponse bias, we found no differences between the responses of early (first-wave) respondents and late (last-wave) respondents for any of the study's hypothesized variables (Kanuk & Berenson, 1975). The FFI serves practitioners who specialize in working with family enterprises, as well as academics studying family enterprises. Our interest is in the role of practitioners who engage primarily in an advisory practice with family enterprises. As such, our hypotheses were only tested using the subsample of self-identified family advisors (n = 253).

Of the 253 mostly completed responses, 159 (63%) were from males and 93 (37%) were from females. The mean age of respondents was 53 years, with the youngest being 22 and the oldest 79. Whites/Caucasians was the largest reported ethnic group (n = 205), followed by Hispanics (n = 33). Overall, respondents were very well educated, with a majority having a master's degree (n = 129), closely followed by bachelor's degree (n = 62) and doctoral degree (n = 52). Respondent's primary occupation consisted of being a family enterprise consultant (n = 96), a family enterprise advisor (n = 66), a family wealth advisor (n = 28), a family wealth consultant (n = 15), and other (n = 42). Most respondents were self-employed (n = 135), with an average of 14 years of work experience with the same company or being self-employed.

The use of a single questionnaire to measure both our independent and dependent variables at one time leads to the potential for common method bias (Podsakoff & Organ, 1986). To alleviate concerns regarding common method bias, we implemented certain procedures in our research design, and we conducted analyses to gauge common method effects. First, we offered our respondents anonymity/confidentiality to diminish the probability of socially desirable responding. Second, respondents were informed that there were no right or wrong answers and were asked to answer the questions truthfully (Podsakoff, MacKenzie, Lee, & Podsakoff, 2003). Third, in our questionnaire design, we proximally separated the independent and dependent variables to reduce the potential effects of common method bias, as well as self-generated validity (Lee & Sukoco, 2010). Third, we subjected all items in our study to a factor analysis (Podsakoff & Organ, 1986), testing for the dimensionality of the data. If a general factor accounting for more than half of the variance emerged, then this could suggest common method bias might affect our results. Using an unrotated principal components factor analysis, the factor analysis produced nine factors, with the first factor accounting for only 23% of the 65% explained variance. Last, with guidance from Podsakoff et al. (2003), a two-phased confirmatory factor analysis was employed to gauge the differences in explained variance between (a) an analysis with the studied latent constructs and (b) the studied latent factor, along with a latent single common method factor (Carlson & Kacmar, 2000). The factor analysis with the common method factor accounted for only 5.8% additionally explained variance compared with the latent factor model consisting of only of the studied constructs—5.8% is well short of the critical threshold of 25% (Williams, Cote, & Buckley, 1989). These results indicate that the effects of common method bias were limited in this study.

Measures

All items were measured on a 7-point Likert-type scale asking respondents the extent to which they agreed or disagreed with each statement and was anchored from 1 = *strongly disagree* to 7 = *strongly agree*. Scale items and factor loadings are presented in the Results section.

Goal Orientation. The three subdimensions of goal orientation (learning orientation, proving orientation, and avoidance orientation) were measured with a 13-item scale developed by Brett and VandeWalle (1999).

Personal Bricolage. Bricolage is creatively combining and recombining existing resources for the purpose of goal accomplishment (Baker & Nelson, 2005; Hmieleski & Corbett, 2006; Senyard et al., in press; Vera, 2002). In our study, the individual's ability to accomplish goals through creatively combining and recombining existing resources is of interest. To investigate this, we modified Senyard et al.'s (in press) bricolage scale to the individual level of analysis. This eight-item scale was selected over other scales (e.g., Hmieleski & Corbett, 2006), as it exclusively focuses on the indicators of bricolage behaviors.

Individual Innovative Behavior. We used a six-item innovative behavior scale adapted from Scott and Bruce (1994) and Yuan and Woodman (2010). In their research, these scholars asked supervisors to rank their subordinates on this scale. As we are studying individuals, who may or may not have supervisors, we asked the respondents to indicate how innovative they perceived themselves to be.

Quality of Feedback. We selected a five-item scale capturing feedback quality drawn from Steelman et al.'s (2004) broader feedback environment scale. The feedback environment scale originally captured feedback quality from supervisors and coworkers. As we were solely interested in the quality of the feedback being derived by the respondent from the family enterprise client, we modified this scale to include phrasing such as "*My clients* give me useful feedback about my job performance" or "I value the feedback I receive *from clients*." A high score on this scale indicates that the feedback received from clients was viewed by the advisor as helpful for understanding and improving performance. Lower scores indicate that the advisor did not perceive feedback from the clients to be as useful.

Data Analyses

To validate the scales through confirmatory factor analysis and test the hypothesized relationships, structural equation modeling (SEM) using LISREL 8.52 was used. Although the primary statistical approach to test for mediation is hierarchical regression modeling (Baron & Kenny, 1986), this study followed the logic and recommendations of other scholars (James, Mulaik, & Brett, 2006; MacKinnon, Lockwood, Hoffman, West, & Sheets, 2002; Schneider, Ehrhart, Mayer, Saltz, & Niles-Jolly, 2005) and used SEM to test Hypotheses 3, 7, and 9. When applying SEM to mediation, two models (i.e., a partially mediated model and a fully mediated model) must be individually tested and the resulting chi-square values compared to indicate whether full mediation occurs. If no statistical difference exists between the resulting chi-square values, the more parsimonious, fully mediated model would be selected (Schneider et al., 2005).

Results

Table 8.1 presents the descriptive statistics, coefficient alphas, and correlation matrix of the studied variables. The coefficient alphas and composite reliabilities were all within acceptable ranges. Some of the correlations among the independent variables were relatively high, suggesting a potential negative impact of multicollinearity. To assess this potential, we examined the correlation matrix for high correlations. The highest correlation ($r = .66$) was between individual innovative behavior and personal bricolage, which was less than the threshold of $r = .80$. Second, we chose to conduct an additional test for multicollinearity through examination of the variance inflation factors. The variance inflation factors were 1.5 or less, which is less than the recommended threshold of 10.0 (Lomax, 1992), indicating that the effects of collinearity were limited.

Before testing the hypotheses, a two-phase confirmatory factor analysis approach was employed to test for measurement invariance on the primary scales, comparing a baseline constrained model with an unconstrained model (Anderson & Gerbing, 1988). Presented in Table 8.2, the completely standardized item factor loadings from the unconstrained model of the six constructs of personal bricolage, individual innovative behavior, learning orientation, proving orientation, avoidance orientation, and quality of feedback ranged from .51 to .87 and were all statistically significant ($p < .05$), with the exception of an item from individual innovative behavior. This item was dropped from statistical analyses, as its loading was .43 and was less than the .50 cutoff. The comparative fit index (CFI), Δ^2 root mean square error of approximation (RMSEA), and standardized root mean residual (SRMR) model fit indices were selected for reporting purposes.

For the second part of the confirmatory process, an unconstrained six-factor model was compared with a six-factor constrained model (i.e., baseline model), in which the paths in the Φ matrix were set to 1. A series of sequential chi-square models revealed that the unconstrained model ($\chi^2 = 849.87$, degrees of freedom [df] = 449; CFI = .95; Δ^2 = .95; RMSEA = .062; SRMR = .068) demonstrated a significantly better fit than the constrained six-factor model ($\chi^2 = 2933.17$, $df = 464$; CFI = .77; Δ^2 = .77; RMSEA = .15; SRMR = .13) based on the chi-square difference test ($\Delta\chi^2 = 2083.30$, $df = 15$; $p < .05$).

As previously mentioned, the loadings ranged from a low of .51 to a high of .87 and were all statistically significant ($p < .05$), indicating convergent validity (Bagozzi & Yi, 1988; Gerbing & Anderson, 1992). Discriminant validity would reveal evidence of the squared intercorrelations between constructs being less than

TABLE 8.1 Descriptive Statistics, Coefficient Alphas, and Correlations of Studied Variables ($n = 231$)

Variable name	M	SD	α	CR	AVE	1	2	3	4	5
1. Personal bricolage	5.68	0.71	.88	.88	.48					
2. Individual innovative behavior	5.69	0.79	.81	.83	.50	.66**				
3. Learning orientation	6.40	0.60	.83	.83	.51	.50**	.55**			
4. Proving orientation	4.64	1.30	.86	.86	.61	.12	.11	.05		
5. Avoidance orientation	3.03	1.23	.82	.81	.51	−.27**	−.19**	−.32**	.20**	
6. Quality of feedback	5.83	0.97	.87	.88	.59	.25**	.26**	.20**	−.14*	−.10

Note. CR = composite reliability; AVE = average variance extracted.

* $p < .05$, two-tailed test; listwise deletion.

** $p < .01$, two-tailed test; listwise deletion.

the average variance extracted (AVE) for each construct (Fornell & Larcker, 1981). Squared intercorrelations were less than the AVE for the respective constructs supporting discriminant validity. Although the AVE for personal bricolage (AVE = .48) was slightly less than the recommended .50 (Fornell & Larcker, 1981), the AVEs for the remainder of the measures were at or greater than .50, which was greater than the recommended threshold.

Before proceeding to hypothesis testing, we considered the impact that the respondent demographic characteristics may have on the results. Specifically, we tested for differences in personal bricolage, individual innovative behavior, learning orientation, proving orientation, avoidance orientation, and quality of feedback based on the demographic variables of respondent gender, age, ethnicity, education, and advisory/consultant role. We found no significant relationships between the demographic variables and the measurements in our model, suggesting that these demographic attributes should not confound our results.

The model fit statistics for the partially mediated model (i.e., fully saturated model) are presented in Table 8.3. The chi-square statistic was significant (χ^2 = 633.52, df = 411; $p < .05$) suggesting that the data did not fit the model well, though this measure is often influenced by sample size and larger correlations in the model (Kelloway, 1998). Given these concerns, we considered other model fit indices, such as CFI (Bentler, 1990), Δ^2 (Bollen, 1989), RMSEA (MacCallum, Browne, & Sugawara, 1996), and SRMR (Hu & Bentler, 1998). Based on these fit indices, the model fits the data well (CFI = .97; Δ^2 = .97; RMSEA = .049; SRMR = .062), and the individual paths of the structural model may be examined. As illustrated in Figure 8.2, Hypothesis 1, which stated that learning orientation should be positively related to quality of feedback, was supported (γ = .27; $p < .05$). For Hypothesis 4, support (γ = −.20; $p < .05$) was found for proving orientation to be negatively related to quality of feedback; however, Hypothesis 5 was not supported (γ = .06; $p > .05$), with avoidance orientation not being negatively related to quality of feedback. A summary of the results for each hypothesis can be found in Table 8.4.

Hypotheses 2a and 2b articulated a direct and positive relationship from learning orientation to the dependent variables of personal bricolage and individual innovative behavior. Support was found for an effect of learning orientation on personal bricolage (γ = .37; $p < .05$) and on individual innovative behavior (γ = .47; $p < .05$). Contrary to Hypotheses 6a and 6b, proving orientation was positively related to personal bricolage (γ = .20; $p < .05$) and to individual innovative behavior (γ = .16; $p < .05$). For Hypotheses 8a and 8b, the findings were mixed, with Hypothesis 8a (i.e., avoidance orientation is negatively related to personal bricolage) accepted (γ = −.20; $p < .05$) and Hypothesis 8b (i.e., avoidance orientation is negatively related to individual innovative behavior) rejected (γ = −.07; $p > .05$).

Multidisciplinary Professional Teams 119

[Figure: Path diagram showing relationships among Learning Orientation (ξ_1), Proving Orientation (ξ_2), Avoidance Orientation (ξ_3), Quality of Feedback (η_1), Personal Bricolage (η_2), and Individual Innovative Behavior (η_3) with the following coefficients:

$\Phi_{31} = .22^*$; $\Phi_{21} = .07$; $\Phi_{32} = -.36^*$
$\gamma_{11} = .27^*$; $\gamma_{12} = -.20^*$; $\gamma_{13} = .06$
$\gamma_{21} = .37^*$; $\gamma_{22} = .20^*$; $\gamma_{23} = -.20^*$
$\gamma_{31} = .47^*$; $\gamma_{32} = .16^*$; $\gamma_{33} = -.07^*$
$\beta_{21} = .26^*$; $\beta_{31} = .24^*$; $\psi_{32} = .42^*$]

Model Fit Statistics: $\chi^2 = 633.52$ (d.f. = 411, $p < 0.005$); CFI = .97; Delta2 (IFI) = .97; RMSEA = .049; SRMR = .062.

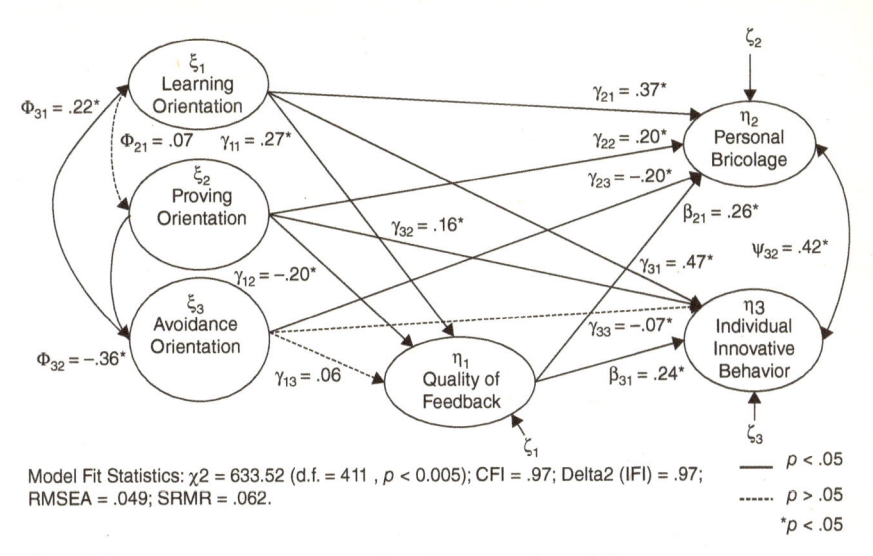

—— $p < .05$
----- $p > .05$
*$p < .05$

FIGURE 8.2 Results of Partially Mediated Structural Model

Hypotheses 3a, 3b, 7a, 7b, 9a, and 9b posited that the quality of feedback would mediate the relationships between the dimensions of goal orientation (learning, proving, avoidance) and adaptive behaviors (bricolage and innovative behavior). For mediation to be present, the goal orientation subdimensions of learning orientation, proving orientation, and avoidance orientation should have a direct linkage to the quality of feedback construct. With the exception of avoidance orientation, learning and proving orientations had significant relationships to quality of feedback. However, the goal orientation subdimensions should not have a statistically significant direct relationship to the corresponding variables of personal bricolage and individual innovative behavior, only an indirect significant relationship through quality of feedback.

To test this approach, a partially mediated model (i.e., fully saturated model; see Table 8.3) was compared with a fully mediated model through a chi-square difference test (Baron & Kenny, 1986; Brown, 1997). In the partially mediated model, the goal orientation subdimension of learning orientation had a direct and significant positive relationship with personal bricolage ($\gamma = .37$; $p < .05$) and with individual innovative behavior ($\gamma = .47$; $p < .05$). Similarly, proving orientation had a significant positive relationship with both personal bricolage ($\gamma = .20$; $p < .05$) and individual innovative behavior ($\gamma = .16$; $p < .05$). Avoidance orientation did have a significant negative relationship with personal bricolage ($\gamma = -.20$; $p < .05$), though it did not have a significant relationship with individual innovative behavior ($\gamma = -.07$; $p > .05$).

TABLE 8.2 Confirmatory Factor Analysis, AVEs, and Construct Reliabilities

Item	Personal bricolage (BRICO)	Individual innovative behavior (INOV)	Learning orientation (LEARN)	Proving orientation (PROVE)	Avoidance orientation (AVOID)	Quality of feedback (QUAL)
By combining my existing resources, I take on a surprising variety of new challenges. (BRICO 1)	.74[a]					
I combine resources to accomplish new challenges that the resources weren't originally intended to accomplish. (BRICO 2)	.72					
I am confident of my ability to find workable solutions to new challenges by using my existing resources. (BRICO 3)	.71					
I take on a broader range of challenges than others with similar resources. (BRICO 4)	.69					
I use any existing resource that seems useful for responding to a new problem or opportunity. (BRICO 5)	.69					
I deal with new challenges by applying a combination of my existing resources and other resources inexpensively available to me. (BRICO 6)	.68					
When I face new challenges, I put together workable solutions from my existing resources. (BRICO 7)	.68					

When dealing with new problems or opportunities, I take action by assuming that I will find a workable solution. (BRICO 8)	.61	
I am innovative. (INOV 1)	.85	
I generate creative ideas. (INOV 2)	.82	
I promote and champion ideas to others. (INOV 3)	.72	
I investigate and secure funds needed to implement new ideas. (INOV 4)	.57	
I search out new technologies, processes, techniques, and/or product ideas. (INOV 5)	.51	
I enjoy challenging and difficult tasks at work where I'll learn new skills. (LEARN 1)		.87
I am willing to select a challenging work assignment that I can learn a lot from. (LEARN 2)		.72
I often look for opportunities to develop new skills and knowledge. (LEARN 3)		.72

(*continued*)

TABLE 8.2 (continued)

Item	Personal bricolage (BRICO)	Individual innovative behavior (INOV)	Learning orientation (LEARN)	Proving orientation (PROVE)	Avoidance orientation (AVOID)	Quality of feedback (QUAL)
I prefer to work in situations that require a high level of ability and talent. (LEARN 4)			.63			
For me, development of my work ability is important enough to take risks. (LEARN 5)			.58			
I try to figure out what it takes to prove my ability to others at work. (PROVE 1)				.87		
I prefer to work on projects where I can prove my ability to others. (PROVE 2)				.80		
I like to show that I can perform better than my coworkers. (PROVE 3)				.78		
I enjoy it when others at work are aware of how well I am doing. (PROVE 4)				.67		
I'm concerned about taking on a task at work if my performance would reveal that I had low ability. (AVOID 1)					.85	
I would avoid taking on a new task if there was a chance that I would appear rather incompetent to others. (AVOID 2)					.70	

Avoiding a show of low ability is more important to me than learning a new skill. (AVOID 3)	.66
I prefer to avoid situations at work where I might perform poorly. (AVOID 4)	.64
The performance feedback I receive from clients is helpful. (QUAL 1)	.86
The feedback I receive from clients helps me do my job. (QUAL 2)	.83
I value the feedback I receive from clients. (QUAL 3)	.75
My clients give me useful feedback about my job performance. (QUAL 4)	.70
The performance information I receive from clients is generally not very helpful. (reverse coded; QUAL 5)	.67

Note. AVE = average variance extracted.

a. Completely standardized factor loading.

The fully mediated model (χ^2 = 691.69, df = 417, $p < .05$; CFI = .96; Δ^2 = .96; RMSEA = .054; SRMR = .12) did not fit the data as well as the partially mediated model (χ^2 = 633.52, df = 411, $p < .05$; CFI = .97; Δ^2 = .97; RMSEA = .049; SRMR = .062). The chi-square difference test ($\Delta\chi^2$ = 58.17, df = 6, $p < .05$) indicated that the partially mediated model fit the data better than the fully mediated model.

Though full mediation is not present, the results do imply the possible presence of partial mediation, with significant relationships from learning orientation to feedback quality and proving orientation to feedback quality. To test for partial mediation, the indirect effects of learning orientation to personal bricolage quality of feedback were assessed. The results indicate that learning orientation (γ = .09; t = 2.73; $p < .05$) had a significant indirect relationship to personal bricolage through quality of feedback, supporting partial mediation. Similarly, learning orientation (γ = .09; t = 2.60; $p < .05$) had a significant indirect relationship to individual innovative behavior through quality of feedback.

Evidence of negative partial mediation through quality of feedback was found for proving orientation to personal bricolage (γ = –.06; t = –2.21; $p < .05$) and to individual innovative behavior (γ = –.06; t = –2.15; $p < .05$). In effect, quality of feedback only partially mediated the relationship of learning orientation to personal bricolage and individual innovative behavior. Comparably, proving orientation to personal bricolage and individual innovative behavior relationships were negatively partially mediated. Given these findings, quality of feedback does not fully mediate the goal orientation to individual innovative behavior or personal bricolage relationships, so Hypotheses 3a, 3b, 7a, and 7b were partially supported, with 9a and 9b not supported. Though the hypotheses for full mediation were rejected, empirical support was found for the direct relationship of quality of feedback to personal bricolage (β = .26; $p < .05$) and to individual innovative behavior (β = .24; $p < .05$).

Discussion and Conclusion

Professional family enterprise advisors assist families in dealing with a range of complex problems, many of which are unique to the family enterprise sector. Given the existence of, and the influential role played by, the family system, most problems are, to an extent, idiosyncratic to the particular family enterprise client. As such, these professionals are required to operate differently than they would in the nonfamily business arena (Levinson, 1983; Strike, 2012). Furthermore, given the nature of the family stakeholders with whom they are dealing, it is likely that family enterprise advisors work in environments where the quality of the feedback from their clients is variable, which increases the potential for task (and outcome) uncertainty. This study attempted to facilitate a better understanding

TABLE 8.3 Structural Model Parameter Estimates for the Partially Mediated Model

Estimates and Fit Statistics	Completely Standardized Estimate	t
Phi parameters		
LEARN ⇔ PROVE	.07	0.93
PROVE ⇔ AVOID	.22*	3.05
LEARN ⇔ AVOID	−.36*	−5.18
Gamma parameters		
LEARN → QUAL	.27*	3.25
PROVE → QUAL	−.20*	−2.64
AVOID → QUAL	.06	0.68
LEARN → BRICO	.37*	4.56
PROVE → BRICO	.20*	2.82
AVOID → BRICO	−.20*	−2.55
LEARN → INOV	.47*	4.93
PROVE → INOV	.16*	2.13
AVOID → INOV	−.07	−0.91
Beta parameters		
QUAL → BRICO	.26*	3.50
QUAL → INOV	.24*	3.03
Psi parameter		
BRICO ⇔ INOV	.42*	4.92
Theta–epsilon parameters[a]		
BRICO 4 ⇔ BRICO 5	.14*	3.81
BRICO 6 ⇔ BRICO 7	.16*	3.81
BRICO 3 ⇔ BRICO 7	.21*	4.88
INOV 2 ⇔ INOV 4	−.08*	−2.40
INOV 1 ⇔ INOV 2	.19*	4.02
INOV 4 ⇔ INOV 5	.10*	1.96
QUAL 1 ⇔ QUAL 4	.12*	2.65
QUAL 2 ⇔ QUAL 4	−.11*	−2.94

Note. Model fit statistics: χ^2 = 633.52 (degrees of freedom = 411, p < .05); comparative fit index = .97; Δ^2 = .97; root mean square error of approximation = .049; standardized root mean residual = .062.

a. The error terms for these indicators were allowed to correlate to improve the overall model fit. Error terms were allowed to correlate only if the terms belonged to the same construct and the modification index score was greater than 10, which is more conservative than the recommended threshold of 5 (Kelloway, 1998). *p < .05, two-tailed test.

of this vital support group to family enterprises. Our findings enable us to offer several observations.

First, the results of our study suggest that family enterprise advisors who have a strong learning orientation will be more likely to acquire feedback from their family enterprise clients. Likewise, these family enterprise advisors are more likely to exhibit behaviors of personal bricolage and individual innovativeness. Importantly, the generation of quality feedback from clients positively enhances how advisors are able to adapt by innovatively recombining their resources. However, an interesting finding of this study is that there was a direct relationship between learning orientation and the individual behaviors of personal bricolage and individual innovative

TABLE 8.4 Summary of Results

Hyothesis	Result
H1: Learning orientation is positively related to feedback quality.	Supported
H2: Learning orientation is positively related to (a) personal bricolage and (b) individual innovative behavior.	H2a: Supported H2b: Supported
H3: The effect of learning orientation on (a) personal bricolage and (b) individual innovative behavior is mediated by feedback quality.	H3a: Partially supported H3b: Partially supported
H4: Proving orientation is negatively related to feedback quality.	Supported
H5: Avoidance orientation is negatively related to feedback quality.	Not supported
H6: Proving orientation is negatively related to (a) personal bricolage and (b) individual innovative behavior.	H6a: Not supported H6b: Not supported
H7: The effect of proving orientation on (a) personal bricolage, and (b) individual innovative behavior is mediated by feedback quality.	H7a: Partially supported H7b: Partially supported
H8: Avoidance orientation is negatively related to (a) personal bricolage and (b) individual innovative behavior.	H8a: Supported H8b: Not supported
H9: The effect of avoidance orientation on (a) personal bricolage and (b) individual innovative behavior is mediated by feedback quality.	H9a: Not supported H9b: Not supported

behavior. This would suggest that although feedback is important, the effect of learning orientation on these behaviors is not completely explained by quality feedback.

Second, proving orientation did not exhibit a negative link with adaptive behaviors. The literature would suggest that there should be a negative relationship between proving orientation and the behaviors we examined. Instead, a positive relationship was observed. This positive relationship is surprising, as the proving orientation was negatively linked to the quality of feedback, as theory would suggest. The quality of feedback acted as a partial negative mediator to advisors' adaptive behaviors. Advisors high in proving orientation who received quality feedback reported diminished ability to adapt by innovatively recombining resources. Conversely, with less feedback, advisors who are proving oriented were positively linked with increased behaviors associated with being bricoleurs and innovators. This finding may be a function of the type of feedback acquired. For instance, persons high in proving orientation often seek out outcome feedback and not process feedback (VandeWalle et al., 2001).

Third, our results indicated that advisors with either a learning orientation or a proving orientation are more likely to engage in adaptive behaviors compared with those high in avoidance orientation. For avoidance orientation, an interesting finding was observed. Although advisors high in avoidance orientation did in fact engage in less adaptive behaviors, this effect could not be explained by the quality of feedback they acquired, as there was no relationship between avoidance orientation and feedback quality. Avoidance orientation is the desire to avoid the demonstration of low ability and the resulting unfavorable judgments associated with poor performance. Persons high in this orientation often avoid challenging roles out of a desire to avoid being critiqued. A similar process may explain why they were less likely to engage in adaptive behaviors, as adaptation involves some risk that the newly adopted behaviors will be unsuccessful.

Overall, this research provides multiple contributions to what we know about family enterprise advisors. Our findings advance the bricolage literature at the individual level and integrate this with other individual level theories of work performance. For instance, the work design literature increasingly emphasizes that individuals can be proactive in defining the nature and boundaries of their work roles (Grant & Parker, 2009). The literature on feedback seeking emphasizes that individuals often seek out performance-related information as a personal resource (Ashford et al., 2003). In this project, we proposed that personal bricolage may be based in part on individuals' ability to acquire and to use feedback in order to be more innovative as they design their own work roles. The results of our study support existing literature showing that feedback plays an important role in work performance, and advance our understanding of how feedback is used in work environments that require adaptivity. In addition, this research extends our understanding of how individuals are able to work on their own. Specifically, our results provide a better appreciation of how individuals self-manage, creatively use, reconfigure, and recombine available resources through personal bricolage and how individual innovative behaviors are applied to personal role management.

In the family enterprise context, the findings from this study improve our perspective on how family enterprise advisors respond to feedback from family enterprise clients. Put simply, advisors who have a learning orientation are more likely to generate quality feedback that enhances their ability to recombine their resources innovatively. Conversely, an advisor who exhibits a proving orientation may seek a minimum amount of feedback, which would increase the importance of feedback that is actually provided by members of the family enterprise.

Also, family enterprise advisors who have a proving orientation may still be effective, even in family enterprises that have a culture of privacy or a tradition of secrecy. Family enterprises have often been characterized as having barriers that are difficult to penetrate (Lester & Cannella, 2006). Family enterprises that consider their enterprise to be "closed" may be better served by advisors who are more proving oriented than learning or avoidance oriented. Advisors who have a proving orientation are often characterized as attempting to demonstrate task competence and to gain favorable judgments from their clients. They may desire little quality feedback to strengthen their ability to be innovative and to use the existing resources around them.

Advisors who have a learning orientation may be less dependent on quality feedback from their family enterprise clients. Advisors with a learning orientation are more likely to observe and to analyze their own task strategies, as well as to experiment with alternative ways to improve task strategies through personal bricolage and individual innovative behaviors. However, family enterprises that engage advisors should strive to provide high feedback quality by engendering trust with family enterprise executives and greater inclusion in family enterprise decisions. If a family enterprise is seeking adaptive problem solving from their advisor and willing to provide quality feedback, then they should focus on hiring advisors with a learning goal orientation.

Implications for Practice

The results of our study indicate that both feedback and goal orientation can have a positive role to play in the advisor–client relationship and that feedback may be the mechanism that links learning and proving orientation to adaptive behaviors. Although our study treated goal orientation as a relatively stable personality trait, there is evidence that individuals can adopt one goal orientation or another depending on the context (Stevens & Gist, 1997). Individuals may be predisposed to have one orientation or the other, but advisors are often adept at choosing their own approaches to goal accomplishment. Advisors may choose to pursue either a learning approach or a proving approach to meeting client needs. From a practitioner standpoint, the following questions may arise: (a) When and how might an advisor choose to adopt a learning orientation as opposed to a proving orientation? (b) What kinds of feedback-seeking behaviors are more likely to lead to the high-quality feedback needed to successfully execute an advising relationship?

The answers to these questions are likely to depend on the complexity of the advising assignment and the "openness" of the family client. Figure 8.3 presents a model of desired advisor approaches to goal orientation and feedback seeking that depend on task complexity and client openness. As discussed earlier, complex tasks require active learning and the acquisition of more complex procedural knowledge for performance to be optimized in the long run. Other tasks, those that are well learned or relatively simple, would be better accomplished with a proving orientation. The "openness" of the family client will determine the extent to which the client provides (or withholds) feedback that might be needed by the advisor. Some clients will be "open" in that they are able and willing to provide feedback about their needs. On the other hand, some clients will be either unwilling or in some cases even unable to provide the advisor with needed feedback. These feedback environments can be viewed as more "closed" in nature.

Complexity of Assignment facing Family Enterprise Advisor

	Closed Family Client	Open Family Client
Complex	Learning Orientation Proactive Feedback Seeking	Learning Orientation Feedback Monitoring (Listening to Cues)
Simple	Proving Orientation Proactive Feedback Seeking	Proving Orientation Feedback Monitoring (Listening to Cues)

Extent of Openness by Family Enterprise Client

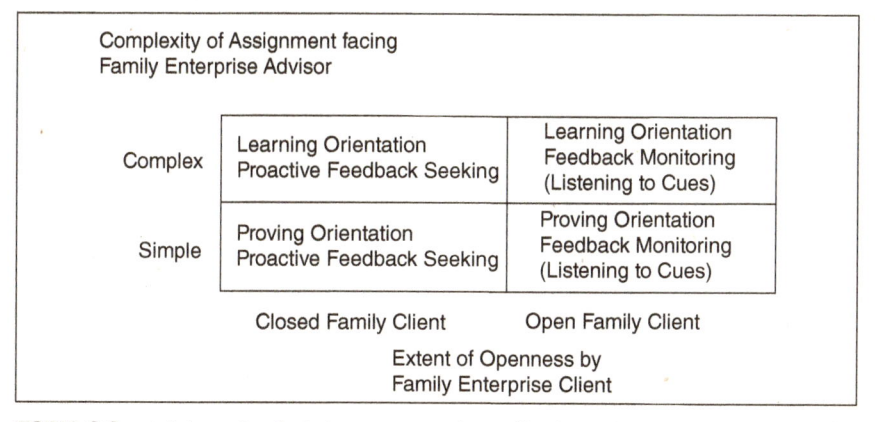

FIGURE 8.3 Advisor Goal Orientation and Feedback Seeking: Approaches Most Useful for Acquiring High-Quality Feedback

There is considerable evidence from the goal orientation literature that learning orientation has its greatest effects on goal accomplishment when tasks are complex and require greater procedural knowledge. In this type of setting, advisors may benefit from taking an approach where they seek to experiment with new ways of serving client needs and take the time to learn from mistakes. This may be especially helpful in long-term advisor–client relationships. Presenting clients with an array of potential solutions to family firm needs, and allowing time for evaluation of these alternative solutions, may lead to more useful feedback and more innovative solutions in the long run. In relatively simple assignments of a shorter duration, a proving orientation might be more appropriate. Here, the advisor is more concerned with delivering a relatively simple solution to a problem as quickly as possible, without a need to learn much more about the problem.

As for actually acquiring feedback when it is needed, a couple of different approaches might be used, and the efficacy of these approaches might vary depending on the willingness of the client to provide information. In an "open" environment, where the family client is freely offering feedback and information to the advisor, it may be more appropriate to simply monitor the feedback environment—or, in other words, to focus on listening to the cues sent by the family client. Active questioning of the client might not be necessary, as the client may already know what information the advisor needs, and provides it freely.

In a "closed" environment, where the family client is reluctant to provide information, or is for some reason shy about providing feedback about the advisor's performance, the advisor may need to be more direct in seeking feedback. Here, an experienced advisor will know the right questions to ask the client and feel comfortable asking those questions directly. Advisors may also need to assess the reasons why a client is "closed." The lack of feedback from a client might not always reflect a "closed" organizational culture or climate but may simply reflect the inexperience of the client or the uncertainty that the client may experience with respect to the information the advisor needs. If the client does not know what feedback to provide, the advisor will need to be proactive in acquiring this information.

Limitations and Future Research

Although the study was useful for establishing links between goal orientation subdimensions and adaptive behaviors, the hypotheses were not fully supported. Future research should investigate other potential mediating mechanisms that could explain the relationship between goal orientation and these types of behaviors. As noted in the introduction, prior research found that goal orientation is related not only to feedback seeking but also to "elaboration" and "rehearsal" of task strategies (Fisher & Ford, 1998; Steele-Johnson et al., 2000). Scholars engaged in future research on personal bricolage and innovative behaviors may wish to pursue a more fine-tuned analysis of how elaboration and rehearsal might facilitate (or hinder) adaptive behavior.

Another potential limitation of this study is the use of only family enterprise advisors, while not sampling their family enterprise clients. In the future, scholars may wish to examine the advisor–client relationship through a dyadic research design to consider the complexities associated with family enterprises (e.g., succession planning, parent–child dynamic, family-centered noneconomic goals). This research would extend the findings presented here by providing a greater understanding of how feedback quality will influence personal bricolage when certain client conditions are prevalent. Likewise, the collection of longitudinal data would provide greater understanding of the process by which these behaviors unfold, as well as provide more valid inferences regarding causality.

Although our study focused on family enterprise advisors as a whole, there may be important differences between advisors that could moderate the relationships observed in this study. Differences in educational background, specialization, and client segments may ultimately lead to different feedback environments, more or less complex advising assignments, and varied opportunities to engage in adaptive behavior. For instance, future research may need to consider the size of the client organization in their research design. The nature of the advisor's role in a large family enterprise may result in different complexities than in a small family enterprise. As another example, family legal advisors are likely to face much different task and role environments than family enterprise advisors, and these different environments may lead to very different feedback. Theoretically meaningful distinctions among different advisor groups may be discovered that ultimately lead to a more sophisticated understanding of how different advisors acquire feedback and subsequently use such feedback for adaptation.

Another limitation of this study is the lack of a direct comparison between family enterprise advisors and advisors who serve nonfamily firms. An assumption, based on the existing family business literature, made in this study is that family enterprise advisors encounter more complexity in their job because of the overlap of family, management, and ownership systems. Scholars may wish to test this assumption, as the extent and nature of this complexity were not established empirically in this study. Furthermore, the nature of the feedback environment encountered by family enterprise advisors also needs further study. Finally, though diagnostic tests indicated little evidence of common method bias, future research may wish to conduct qualitative interviews through field research or the inclusion of secondary data to further increase confidence in the inferences we make here.

Conclusion

In conclusion, we have endeavored to understand family enterprise advisors by examining how their goal orientation is linked to personal bricolage and individual innovative behavior. Our findings indicate that quality of feedback can play an important role in this process. Though it does not fully mediate the goal orientation to behavior relationship, it does partially mediate these relationships. As family enterprises seek out family enterprise advisors for future endeavors, both parties should be cognizant of how the two parties are interrelated and the nature of their interdependent relationship affects the adaptivity of the advisor to client needs. Given the heterogeneity of the family enterprise sector and the variety of the tasks and environments that advisors undertake, advisors and clients may choose different approaches to their relationship depending on the complexity of the assignment and the openness of the client. Interactions with family stakeholders, and the subsequent openness to provide feedback, would likely vary by assignment. This may determine the choice of advisor, have a bearing on the relationship, and, ultimately, affect the outcome.

Declaration of Conflicting Interests

The author(s) declared no potential conflicts of interest with respect to the research, authorship, and/or publication of this article.

Funding

The author(s) received no financial support for the research, authorship, and/or publication of this article.

Notes

1. In this article, we use the term *advisors* to include the FFI professional categories of family enterprise consultants, family enterprise advisors, family wealth advisors, and family wealth consultants.

References

Aldrich, H. E., & Cliff, J. E. (2003). The pervasive effects of family on entrepreneurship: Toward a family embeddedness perspective. *Journal of Business Venturing, 18*, 573–596.

Anderson, J. C., & Gerbing, D. W. (1988). Structural equation in practice: A review and recommended two-step approach. *Psychological Bulletin, 103*, 411–423.

Arregle, J. L., Hitt, M. A., Sirmon, D. G., & Very, P. (2007). The development of organizational social capital: Attributes of family firms. *Journal of Management Studies, 44*, 73–95.

Ashford, S. J. (1986). Feedback-seeking in individual adaptation: A resource perspective. *Academy of Management Journal, 29*, 465–487.

Ashford, S. J., Blatt, R., & VandeWalle, D. (2003). Reflections on the looking glass: A review of research on feedback-seeking behavior in organizations. *Journal of Management, 29*, 773–799.

Ashford, S. J., & Cummings, L. L. (1983). Feedback as an individual resource: Personal strategies of creating information. *Organizational Behavior and Human Performance, 32*, 370–398.

Bagozzi, R. P., & Yi, Y. (1988). On the evaluation of structural equation models. *Journal of the Academy of Marketing Science, 16*, 74–94.

Baker, T., & Nelson, R. E. (2005). Creating something from nothing: Resource construction through entrepreneurial bricolage. *Administrative Science Quarterly, 50*, 329–366.

Bammens, Y., Voordeckers, W., & Gils, A. V. (2008). Boards of directors in family firms: A generational perspective. *Small Business Economics, 31*, 163–180.

Baron, R. M., & Kenny, D. A. (1986). The moderator-mediator variable distinction in social psychological research: Conceptual, strategic, and statistical considerations. *Journal of Personality and Social Psychology, 51*, 1173–1182.

Bentler, P. M. (1990). Comparative fit indexes in structural equation modeling. *Psychological Bulletin, 107*, 238–246.

Bollen, K. A. (1989). *Structural equations with latent variables.* New York, NY: John Wiley.

Brett, J. F., & VandeWalle, D. (1999). Goal orientation and goal content as predictors of performance in a training program. *Journal of Applied Psychology, 84*, 863–873.

Brown, R. L. (1997). Assessing specific mediational effects in complex theoretical models. *Structural Equation Modeling, 4*, 142–156.

Carlson, D. S., & Kacmar, K. M. (2000). Work–family conflict in the organization: Do life role values make a difference? *Journal of Management, 26*, 1031–1054.

Chua, J., Chrisman, J. J., & Sharma, P. (1999). Defining the family business by behavior. *Entrepreneurship Theory and Practice, 23*(4), 19–39.

Cusella, L. P. (1987). Feedback, motivation, and performance. In F. M. Jablin, L. L. Putnam, K. H. Roberts, & L. W. Porter (Eds.), *Handbook of organizational communication* (pp. 624–678). Newbury Park, CA: Sage.

Danes, S. M. (2011). Pillow talk leaks: Integrating couple interactions into entrepreneurship research. *Entrepreneurship Research Journal, 1.* Retrieved from http://www.degruyter.com/view/j/erj

Davis, P. S., & Harveston, P. D. (1999). In the founder's shadow: Conflict in the family firm. *Family Business Review, 12*, 311–323.

Davis, W. D., Carson, C., Ammeter, A., & Treadway, D. (2005). The interactive effects of goal orientation and feedback specificity on task performance. *Human Performance, 18*, 409–426.

DeShon, R., & Gillespie, J. (2005). A motivated action theory account of goal orientation. *Journal of Applied Psychology, 90*, 1096–1127.

Dillman, D. A., Smyth, J. D., & Christian, L. M. (2009). *Internet, mail, and mixed-mode surveys: The tailored design method.* Englewood Cliffs, NJ: Wiley.

Dweck, C. S. (1986). Motivational processes affecting learning. *American Psychologist, 41,* 1040–1048.

Dweck, C. S., & Leggett, E. L. (1988). A social-cognitive approach to motivation and personality. *Psychological Review, 95,* 256–273.

Eddleston, K. A., & Kellermanns, F. W. (2007). Destructive and productive family relationships: A stewardship theory perspective. *Journal of Business Venturing, 22,* 545–565.

Elliot, A. J., & Harackiewicz, J. M. (1996). Approach and avoidance achievement goals and intrinsic motivation: A mediational analysis. *Journal of Personality and Social Psychology, 70,* 461–475.

Fisher, S. L., & Ford, J. K. (1998). Differential effects of learner effort and goal orientation on two learning outcomes. *Personnel Psychology, 51,* 397–420.

Fornell, C., & Larcker, D. F. (1981). Evaluation structural equation models with unobservable variables and measurement error. *Journal of Marketing Research, 18,* 39–50.

Gerbing, D. W., & Anderson, J. C. (1992). Monte Carlo evaluations of goodness of fit indices for structural equation models. *Sociological Methods & Research, 21,* 132–60.

Goodman, J. M. (1998). Defining the new professional: The family business counsellor. *Family Business Review, 11,* 349–354.

Goodman, J. S., Wood, R. E., & Hendrickx, M. (2004). Feedback specificity, exploration, and learning. *Journal of Applied Psychology, 89,* 248–262.

Grant, A. M., & Parker, S. K. (2009). Redesigning work design theories: The rise of relational and proactive perspectives. *Academy of Management Annals, 3,* 317–375.

Hirst, G., Van Knippenberg, D., & Zhou, J. (2009). A cross-level perspective on employee creativity: Goal orientation, team learning behavior, and individual creativity. *Academy of Management Journal, 52,* 280–293.

Hmieleski, K. M., & Corbett, A. C. (2006). Proclivity for improvisation as a predictor of entrepreneurial intentions. *Journal of Small Business Management, 44,* 45–63.

Hu, L., & Bentler, P. M. (1998). Fit indices in covariance structure modeling: Sensitivity to underparameterized model misspecification. *Psychological Methods, 3,* 424–453.

Ilgen, D. R., Fisher, C. D., & Taylor, M. S. (1979). Consequences of individual feedback on behavior in organizations. *Journal of Applied Psychology, 64,* 349–371.

Jaffe, D. T., & Lane, S. H. (2004). Sustaining a family dynasty: Key issues facing complex multigenerational business and investment-owning families. *Family Business Review, 17,* 81–98.

James, L. R., Mulaik, S. A., & Brett, J. M. (2006). A tale of two methods. *Organizational Research Methods, 9,* 233–244.

Kanfer, R., & Ackerman, P. (1989). Motivation and cognitive abilities: An integrative aptitude-treatment interaction approach to skill acquisition. *Journal of Applied Psychology, 74,* 657–690.

Kanuk, L., & Berenson, C. (1975). Mail surveys and response rates: A literature review. *Journal of Marketing Research, 22,* 440–453.

Kelloway, E. K. (1998). *Using LISREL for structural equation modeling: A researcher's guide.* Thousand Oaks, CA: Sage.

Kluger, A. N., & DeNisi, A. (1996). The effects of feedback interventions on performance: A historical review, meta-analysis and a preliminary feedback intervention theory. *Psychological Bulletin, 119,* 254–284.

Lee, L. Y., & Sukoco, B. M. (2010). The effects of cultural intelligence on expatriate performance: The moderating effects of international experience. *International Journal of Human Resource Management, 21,* 963–981.

Lester, R. H., & Cannella, A. A., Jr. (2006). Interorganizational familiness: How family firms use interlocking directorates to build community-level social capital. *Entrepreneurship Theory and Practice, 30,* 755–775.

Levinson, H. (1983). Consulting with family businesses: What to look for, what to look out for. *Organizational Dynamics, 12,* 71–80.

Locke, E. A., & Latham, G. D. (1990). *A theory of goal setting and task performance.* Englewood Cliffs, NJ: Prentice Hall.

Lomax, R. G. (1992). *Statistical concepts: A second course for education and the behavioral sciences.* White Plains, NY: Longman.

MacCallum, R. C., Browne, M. W., & Sugawara, H. M. (1996). Power analysis and determination of sample size for covariance structure modeling. *Psychological Methods, 1,* 130–149.

MacKinnon, D. P., Lockwood, C. M., Hoffman, J. M., West, S. G., & Sheets, V. (2002). A comparison of methods to test mediation and other intervening variables effects. *Psychological Methods, 7,* 83–104.

Mitchell, R. K., Morse, E., & Sharma, P. (2003). The transacting cognitions of nonfamily employees in the family businesses setting. *Journal of Business Venturing, 18,* 533–551.

Neck, C. P., & Manz, C. C. (1996). Total leadership quality: Integrating employee self-leadership and total quality management. In D. B. Fedor & S. Ghosh (Eds.), *Advances in the management of organizational quality* (Vol. 1., pp. 39–78). Greenwich, CT: JAI Press.

Nicholson, H., Shepherd, D., & Woods, C. (2010). Advising New Zealand's family businesses: Current issues and opportunities. *University of Auckland Business Review, 12*, 1–7.

Podsakoff, P., MacKenzie, S., Lee, J., & Podsakoff, N. (2003). Common method biases in behavioral research: A critical review of the literature and recommended remedies. *Journal of Applied Psychology, 88*, 879–903.

Podsakoff, P. M., & Organ, D. L. (1986). Self-reports in organizational research: Problems and prospects. *Journal of Management, 12*, 531–544.

Porath, C., & Bateman, T. (2006). Self-regulation: From goal orientation to job performance. *Journal of Applied Psychology, 91*, 185–192.

Schneider, B., Ehrhart, M. G., Mayer, D. M., Saltz, J. L., & Niles-Jolly, K. (2005). Understanding organization-customer links in service settings. *Academy of Management Journal, 48*, 1017–1032.

Scott, S. G., & Bruce, R. A. (1994). Determinants of innovative behavior: A path model of individual innovation in the workplace. *Academy of Management Journal, 37*, 580–607.

Seijts, G., Latham, G., Tasa, K., & Latham, B. (2004). Goal setting and goal orientation: An integration of two different yet related literatures. *Academy of Management Journal, 47*, 227–240.

Senyard, J. M., Baker, T., & Davidsson, P. (in press). Bricolage as a path to innovativeness for resource-constrained new firms. *Journal of Product Innovation Management*.

Steele-Johnson, D., Beauregard, R., Hoover, P., & Schmidt, A. (2000). Goal orientation and task demand effects on motivation, affect, and performance. *Journal of Applied Psychology, 85*, 724–738.

Steelman, L. A., Levy, P. E., & Snell, A. F. (2004). The feedback environment scale (FES): Construct definition, measurement and validation. *Educational and Psychological Measurement, 64*, 165–184.

Stevens, C. K., & Gist, M. E. (1997). Effects of self-efficacy and goal-orientation training on negotiation skill maintenance: What are the mechanisms? *Personnel Psychology, 50*, 955–978.

Strike, V. M. (2012). Advising the family firm: Reviewing the past to build the future. *Family Business Review, 25*, 156–177.

Tagiuri, R., & Davis, J. A. (1996). Bivalent attributes of the family firm. *Family Business Review, 9*, 199–208.

Upton, N., Vinton, K., Seaman, S., & Moore, C. (1993). Research note: Family business consultants—Who we are, what we do, and how we do it. *Family Business Review, 6*, 301–311.

VandeWalle, D. (1997). Development and validation of a work domain goal orientation instrument. *Educational and Psychological Measurement, 57*, 995–1015.

VandeWalle, D., Cron, W., & Slocum, J. (2001). The role of goal orientation following performance feedback. *Journal of Applied Psychology, 86*, 629–640.

VandeWalle, D., & Cummings, L. L. (1997). A test of the influence of goal orientation on the feedback-seeking process. *Journal of Applied Psychology, 82*, 390–400.

Vera, D. M. (2002). *Improvisation and its impact on performance* (Unpublished doctoral dissertation). University of Western Ontario, London, Ontario, Canada.

White, P. E. (2007). Hidden dragons: Handling family conflicts in buy-sell agreements for business succession. *Journal of Financial Planning, 20*, 70–76.

Williams, L. J., Cote, J. A., & Buckley, M. R. (1989). Lack of method variance in self-reported affect and perceptions of work: Reality or artifact? *Journal of Applied Psychology, 74*, 462–468.

Yuan, F., & Woodman, R. W. (2010). Innovative behavior in the workplace: The role of performance and image outcome expectations. *Academy of Management Journal, 53*, 323–342.

Author Biographies

Walter D. Davis is an Associate Professor of Management at the University of Mississippi. His research interests include employee proactivity, self-management, goal orientation, and strategic human resource management. His articles have been published in journals such as *Journal of Management*, *Personnel Psychology*, *Journal of Organizational Behavior*, *Human Performance*, *Leadership Quarterly*, and *Group and Organization Management*.

Clay Dibrell is an Associate Professor of Management at the University of Mississippi. His research has been published in leading academic journals, including *Entrepreneurship Theory and Practice*, *Family Business Review*, *Journal of Small Business Management*, *Small Business Economics*, and *Journal of Family Business Strategy*. He is an Associate Editor of *Journal of Family Business Strategy* and an editorial board member of *Family Business Review*.

Justin Craig is an Associate Professor of Entrepreneurship at Northeastern University in Boston. His research has been published in leading academic journals, including *Journal of Business Venturing*, *Entrepreneurship Theory and Practice*, *Family Business Review*, *Journal of Business Research*, *Journal of Small Business Management*, *Small Business Economics*, *Journal of Family Business Strategy*, and *Journal of World Business*, among others. He has been an Associate Editor of *Family Business Review* since 2010.

Judy Green is the President of the Family Firm Institute. She holds a PhD in aesthetics and education from Marquette University.

ASSESSMENT TEST 8

It is now time to test your knowledge using the interactive assessment tool available online at www.familyenterprisebook.com/self-assessments. Enter "familyenterprise" as your password to proceed with the individual assessment. Your responses will be automatically scored and, in the event that you have entered an incorrect response, the correct answer will be provided.

1. Choose all responses that apply: Professionals engaged by a family enterprise are accountable for:
   - ☐ The recommendations they make.
   - ☐ Understanding the systemic implications of their recommendations.
   - ☐ Gathering data from the critical players.
   - ☐ None of the above.

2. Choose all responses that apply: Which of the following do family enterprise professionals need to focus on as they collaborate with others offering professional services?
   - ☐ What the other professionals are recommending.
   - ☐ What the other professionals' relationships are or have been with the client.
   - ☐ The needs and values of the individuals in each of the three circles.
   - ☐ How assessments may differ from professional to professional.
   - ☐ How to show the client that he or she has more to offer than the other professionals.
   - ☐ None of the above.

3. Choose all responses that apply: A successful multidisciplinary team has the following attributes or goals:
   - ☐ Working together with the client to find a solution for the problems presented.
   - ☐ An ability to reach consensus effectively.
   - ☐ An understanding of what each member has to offer.
   - ☐ None of the above.

4. Choose all responses that apply: The types of multidisciplinary teams working with family enterprises are:
   ☐ Consulting.
   ☐ Collaborative.
   ☐ Accidental.
   ☐ Dysfunctional.
   ☐ None of the above.

5. True or False: Multidisciplinary teams require additional work team building by the consultants and advisors involved.

6. True or False: Boundaries, process/content, and finances are the three areas that affect the relationships of the team members and must be addressed before the engagement begins.

7. True or False: Family enterprises want to be able to coordinate and integrate the advice and work of the team themselves.

8. True or False: A collaborative team is one in which the advisors have not previously worked together and meet instead through the client.

9. True or False: The main reason for multidisciplinary teamwork is to save the client money.

10. True or False: Management consultants are located in the middle of the process-content continuum.

CHAPTER 9

Applying What You Have Learned

Using a multidisciplinary approach, this study has sought to introduce and establish a cutting-edge framework for all those working with and within family enterprise. In closing, three actual cases are presented.

Read each case carefully. Then use the body of knowledge and tools of analysis mastered in the previous chapters to think through the complexities and nuances of each case. Consider how, from your particular profession vis-à-vis family enterprise—or, perhaps, your own position within such an enterprise—you might address each case. Once you have done so, read the Postscript material that follows each case to see how, in fact, the challenges facing the family enterprise were resolved.

CASE 1

Two brothers have been in the lighting supply business for more than thirty years. Their 50/50 partnership has been filled with success, trust, respect, fairness, equality, and open communication. Older brother Martin (age 63), has one son, Kevin (age 33), who is a buyer and has been with the company for 10 years. Younger brother Arnold (age 59), has two sons—Leo (age 34) and Harry (age 30)—both of whom have been with the company for approximately the same period of time. Leo oversees operations, while Harry handles sales. Martin and Arnold feel it is time to plan for ownership transfer. All three of the younger generation members are capable, hard workers and contribute equally to the company. The fathers have arranged a meeting with their accountant and attorney. They agreed to freeze retained earnings 50/50. Now they wish to explore how they might divide the stock moving forward, with 33 percent to each of the younger generation members or 50 percent to Martin's son and 25 percent each to Arnold's sons.

Consider how you might handle such a case. In particular, focus on the potential desires, concerns, and expectations of each family member here. What systems concepts and/or theoretical frameworks might be most relevant in this case?

Go to *www.familyenterprisebook.com* and enter the password *"familyenterprise"* to see what the family decided.

CASE 2

Pat (age 37) and Jody (age 38) are siblings in their family's chain of computer sales and service centers. Both have high-quality MBAs and both entered the business at approximately the same time. Each is a capable leader and has achieved significant success, as evidenced in their equally contributing divisions of the company. Yet their styles are rather different. Pat is introverted, a planner, strong on detail and follow through. Jody, by contrast, is more extroverted and creative; she also possesses excellent interpersonal skills. Though they move in different circles, they have always been fairly competitive with one another. Their father, who is president and founder of the company, wants to address succession issues. In his mind, the choice of a future owner is clear. Since ultimately Pat and Jody will each own 50 percent of the common stock, all have agreed to create a Board of Advisors to act as tie-breakers in case there is a major disagreement between the siblings. The succession of leadership, however, is a bit more complex. Both Pat and Jody have lobbied their father in attempt to position themselves to be the next leader of the enterprise. Every so often their father mentions the notion of co-leadership, but he wants his children to decide between themselves. Yet they seem to want him to decide.

As in the previous case, begin your analysis with a consideration of the core issues here and how best to address them. What concepts, systems theoretical insights, and/or governance issues are emerging here?

Go to *www.familyenterprisebook.com* and enter the password *"familyenterprise"* to see what the family decided.

CASE 3

Bernie and Irwin Wheeler own a chain of distribution centers and are an unbeatable father-son partnership. Because of their business success and uncommonly close relationship, they attract national prominence and are the envy of their industry. After six months of negotiations, they acquired a distributorship in an abutting territory that increased their business by 30 percent. Now, two months later, they are suddenly presented with the opportunity to acquire another abutting distributor that is on the verge of bankruptcy. This acquisition would instantly double their business and position them as one of their industry's largest distributors. Bernie (age 60) is president of the company and still the entrepreneur. Son Irwin (age 31) has been with his father for seven years and serves as Chief Operating Officer. While desirous of growth, he is more cautious than his father. Retained earnings have grown steadily through the past decade and, for the first time in recent years, the company requires modest debt to finance its growing inventory and receivables from the first acquisition. Another acquisition would be a great opportunity for increased sales and market control, but would also require a substantial further increase in inventory and receivables. Bernie and Irwin both think the income pro formas look good. But Irwin is concerned. He is not sure that such a major risk is right for the company at this point. Bernie, meanwhile, feels that this is the opportunity of a lifetime and is convinced that the acquisition is the right move. He has expressed total confidence in Irwin's ability to manage the growth. Bernie's and Irwin's accountant and trusted advisor, Albert, is called upon, and Irwin shares his lingering doubts. As he questions the wisdom of a second acquisition at this time, Irwin also wonders whose decision this ought to be, Bernie's or his.

Among a variety of other issues and challenges, this final case invites you to explore in some detail the role of the trusted advisor in family enterprise. It also opens the door to the application of what has been learned about process and content. Consider how you might begin to sort the issues here from the perspective of each family member, as well as using the theoretical frameworks discussed earlier in this book.

Go to *www.familyenterprisebook.com* and enter the password *"familyenterprise"* to see what the family decided.

Glossary

accidental team: A team of advisors who meet and connect through the client only.

advisors: Includes those professionals who view themselves as family business advisors and family wealth advisors. They continue to work mainly in their profession or origin.

aligning: Achieving balance of interests of family and owners, and of owners and the enterprise, and the enterprise and the family.

authority: The right to control, command, decide, or determine, usually established formally by a legal document or requirement. There is also informal authority within a family enterprise that may be established by practice over time, based on factors such as age, parenting, gender, sibling birth sequence, and strength of individual personality.

balancing point: An analytical model that shows key points of connection among systems in a family enterprise, emphasizing the importance of having a person or group maintain communication and/or resolve differences in interests among owners, families, and managers.

behavioral science professional: This professional works at the intersection of psychology and interpersonal relations, and its application for successful family and working relationships.

board of advisors: A group of informal advisors with no fiduciary responsibility and no formal power to make decisions, but available to the founder for advice.

board of directors: A group of individuals (with fiduciary and formal power) elected by shareholders to establish corporate management policies, select top management and make decisions on basic issues, such as dividend policies, mergers and acquisitions, sale of the enterprise or major assets.

boundary: Refers to the quality of the connection and the separation between the components of a system, or between and among systems. A boundary is not a barrier, but, like a healthy cell membrane, is semipermeable and regulates the exchange of substances, energy, information, emotions, and values between components and systems.

client: In a broad sense the client is closely related to a "customer," someone purchasing or receiving benefits from an enterprise. In multidisciplinary approaches to advising and consulting, people from differing professional backgrounds will have differing definitions, ethical, practical, and legal, of who is or can be the client. If various professionals are working together in a multidisciplinary team, they will have to have the understanding of the client resolved before the work begins.

collaborative team: A multidisciplinary team made up of advisors from different disciplines who get to know each other's work, and bring each other into client situations on an as-needed basis.

consultants: Includes family business consultants and family wealth consultants who tend to have a balanced process/content focus and help integrate the plans and interactions of the family, ownership, and management groups as well as the individuals within each group; typically they no longer practice in their profession of origin.

consulting firm: A firm that is comprised of multidisciplinary professionals who work together on a regular basis.

controlling ownership: A term used in the development model to refer to the stage where a single person or couple controls operations and ownership of an enterprise; can also refer to the group that controls ownership, such as the majority of shareholders.

core disciplines of family enterprise professionals: The original professional field of study and training of family enterprise consultants and advisors, for example, law, finance, management science, or behavioral science

cousin consortium: A term used in the development model to refer to the stage where ownership is held by family members from different branches of the family, such as cousins; often this stage occurs when a family enterprise has transitioned from the second generation to the third generation.

development model: A version of the three-circle model, modified to include the dimension of time, which illustrates how enterprise, ownership, and family are connected and change over time in response to changes in individual or group interests, needs, responsibilities, and structures.

dysfunctional team: A team in which advisors are working for the same client, and work with little to no coordination between them.

entrepreneur: A person who initiates, organizes, and manages any enterprise, especially a business, usually with considerable initiative and risk.

estate planner: A professional who provides advice regarding what happens to various resources upon the death of the client, and steps to be taken during the client's life to structure the resources in a manner that accomplishes the goals of the client.

evaluation: The act of describing the strengths and weaknesses of the systems and the members of the systems, within a family enterprise, including their competencies, structures, and procedures; to be distinguished from valuation, which is a formal appraisal process.

executive coach: An advisor and/or consultant who focuses on the needs of top-level management of an enterprise and who works closely with individuals in leadership positions to accomplish certain objectives, both individual and organizational.

family business: It may consist of one or more activities, such as an operating business only; alternatively, the enterprise might include real estate leased to the business. Another possible configuration is an operating business with a diversified wealth portfolio held for the benefit of the family, often referred to as a family office.

family business advisor: A professional, often with multiple areas of expertise, but operating essentially out of a core discipline, who assists family enterprises to accomplish their goals and objectives.

family council: A body of family governance composed of family members that assists in developing structures, policies, and procedures needed by the family; designed to achieve the family's goals, improve communications, inform and educate, and oversee its business and investments.

family enterprises: An economic venture in which two or more members of a family have a commitment to and financial interest in ownership and usually an expectation of the continuation of the enterprise; nonfamily members are also involved in family enterprises.

family governance: The way that the family is organized to make decisions about its current and future stewardship, ownership, and oversight of its various family enterprises.

family office: A separate entity apart from the operating business (and sometimes created with the assets realized after the sale of a family enterprise) consisting of a diversified wealth portfolio held for the benefit of the family.

family system: A system comprised of family members that makes decisions and interacts with the other systems of the family enterprise.

financial professionals: Employed by a family enterprise to identify, record, and verify financial data; determine cash needed by the owners and business and how to invest that cash; obtain and maintain access to cash; ensure cash is available in a catastrophic situation, such as death or natural disaster.

formal systems: Those systems that are typically written down, such as accounting procedures, governing structures, voting arrangements.

foundation: An institution financed by a donation or legacy to aid research, education, the arts, and so on. Some foundations are begun by families that have acquired assets from a family enterprise and want to use these assets to further the family's philanthropic goals.

Glossary

founder: The entrepreneur who first creates an enterprise that may or may not become a family enterprise depending on the extent to which other family members are brought in as employees, managers, or owners.

governance system: A system of structures and processes of authority, accountability, and influence that are, in family enterprises, interconnected. These various governance structures organize and oversee the systems of families, owners, and business. They can include family councils, boards of directors, shareholder assemblies, and family offices.

homeostasis: The ability of any living system to maintain a degree of stability while still being able to adapt and change.

informal systems: Implied but not recorded systems, such as an organization's culture or its method of dealing with conflict.

interdependence: Mutual dependence; in a family enterprise the individual's need for independence needs to be balanced against various aspects of interdependence.

legal professionals: Employed by a family enterprise to structure the enterprise in compliance with laws and regulations, to establish and change agreements, to work with individuals in their estate and tax plans, and to deal with conflicts both within the enterprise and between the enterprise and outside entities.

legal structure: An entity recognized in law for having certain essential elements of governance, accountability, and relationships among categories of those most closely involved with the enterprise. Major categories of such structures are: corporations (owned by shareholders, who select the board of directors, who select management); partnerships (ownership, policy, and management shared by two or more people); and trusts (beneficiaries entitled to the beneficial interests, which are managed by a trustee or trustees).

legal system: Societal way of creating and enforcing agreements and resolving disputes if individuals do not agree; system allows individuals and groups to create an agreement or other legal arrangement to make legally enforceable all or parts of a family enterprise. The legal requirements for an enterprise are generally shaped by government laws and regulations.

management science professionals: Employed to create, evaluate, and suggest changes to current systems with services such as organizational development, communication, business planning, management development, leadership development, human resource development, strategic planning, and compensation policies.

multidisciplinary team: A group of professionals working for a family who communicate, follow an agreed-upon plan, and share what they are doing with each other and the client.

multigenerational families: Families in which two or more generations of family members participate in the family enterprise.

ownership forum: Made up exclusively of owners, a structure that is set up to discuss issues specific to owners of the enterprise.

ownership group: Typically a subset (or subsets) of the family group, including individuals or entities (such as other businesses or trusts) owning the enterprise.

partnership: When the ownership is shared and formalized in a partnership.

perception filters: How the perspectives of the various professionals from the core disciplines shape work done with a family enterprise. For example, an attorney may view the issues involved with a family enterprise only from a legal perspective, an accountant from an accounting perspective, and so on.

personne de confiance: Equivalent of the trusted advisor.

process/content: Process refers to how something is done or said; content to what is done or said. The process/content framework refers to the examination of how and when each is used in working with and in family enterprises.

scapegoat: A person or group made to bear the blame for others.

sibling partnership: A term used in the development model to refer to the stage when ownership has passed to a succeeding generation consisting of siblings.

stakeholders: Individuals or groups holding a direct or indirect interest in an enterprise; can be internal to the enterprise—for example, board members, management, employees—or external, such as shareholders, customers, government, vendors, unions.

stewardship: Owners who behave as stewards and feel a responsibility to pass on roughly the same amount, or greater, wealth and capital to the next generation. In a broader sense, it is a willingness to be accountable to and for an entity or ideal larger than oneself, a business, a family legacy, or a community.

succession planning: The process and content of preparing for a successful transition of leadership in a family enterprise, often from one generation to the next.

system: An entity that involves how individuals or groups organize their communication, relationships, structures, policies, and procedures; an arrangement of people, structures, or things that function together as a unit; can be formal or informal, deliberate or accidental, conscious or unconscious, prescribed or evolutionary.

system dynamics: History or pattern of change, development, and growth of systems.

systems theory: A holistic explanatory model that recognizes that all parts of a system are interdependent and that the actions of one group impact other groups in the system.

three-circle model: An analytical model that portrays the interacting and interdependent roles of family, enterprise, and ownership, with boundaries often unclear as one individual may be part of two or three circles wearing different hats at different times and for different purposes.

transition: Any major shift in leadership or a system, often occurring after death or retirement; can be from one sibling to another but most often refers to the change from one generation to the next in the evolution of a family enterprise.

triangling: The tendency of two people who are unable to resolve a conflict, or who are experiencing distress in a relationship, to involve a third person, entity, or process.

trusted advisor: Has a special personal advisory relationship with the client in which he/she provides a perspective on any topic that the client desires; usually based in one of the main professions of origin but evolved over time into a relationship of trust and confidence in areas that extend beyond the advisor's major area. This is the person to whom the client turns for advice regarding major issues and decisions and may change over time.

valuation: A formal appraisal of the monetary worth of an enterprise or one of more of its components, conducted by a firm or individual with expertise in accounting, investment, and other elements of the field of finance. The expert will typically analyze past trends and future expectations in revenues and expenses; returns on investment; assets and liabilities shown on balance sheets; and competition, regulatory framework, and other aspects of the broader economic environment of the enterprise.

values: The deepest ideals an individual or group holds as qualities that are considered excellent, useful, or desirable.

Suggested Readings from Family Business Review: Journal of the Family Firm Institute

CLASSICS

Aronoff, Craig E., and John L. Ward. "Family-Owned Businesses: A Thing of the Past or a Model for the Future?" *Family Business Review* 8, no. 2 (June 1995).

Danco, Leon A., and John L. Ward. "Beyond Success: The Continuing Contribution of the Family Foundation." *Family Business Review* 3, no. 4 (December 1990).

Harris, Dawn, Jon I. Martinez, and John L. Ward. "Is Strategy Different for the Family-Owned Business?" *Family Business Review* 7, no. 2 (June 1994).

Ward, John L. "Growing the Family Business: Special Challenges and Best Practices." *Family Business Review* 10, no. 4 (December 1997).

Ward, John L., and Christina Dolan. "Defining and Describing Family Business Ownership Configurations." *Family Business Review* 11, no. 4 (December 1998).

RECENT OVERVIEW ARTICLES

Chrisman, James J., Franz W. Kellermanns, Kam C. Chan, and Kartono Liano. "Intellectual Foundations of Current Research in Family Business: An Identification and Review of 25 Influential Articles." *Family Business Review* 23, no. 1 (March 2010).

Gupta, Vipin, and Nancy Levenburg. "A Thematic Analysis of Cultural Variations in Family Businesses: The CASE Project." *Family Business Review* 23, no. 2 (June 2010).

James, Albert E., Jennifer E. Jennings, and Rhonda S. Breitkreuz. "Worlds Apart?: Rebridging the Distance Between Family Science and Family Business Research." *Family Business Review* 25, no. 1 (March 2012).

Jimenez, Rocio Martinez. "Research on Women in Family Firms: Current Status and Future Directions." *Family Business Review* 22, no. 1 (March 2009).

Rothausen, Teresa J. "Management Work—Family Research and Work—Family Fit: Implications for Building Family Capital in Family Business." *Family Business Review* 22, no. 3 (September 2009).

Salvato, Carlo, and Ken Moores. "Research on Accounting in Family Firms: Past Accomplishments and Future Challenges." *Family Business Review* 23, no. 3 (September 2010).

Stewart, Alex, and Michael A. Hitt. "Why Can't a Family Business Be More Like a Nonfamily Business?: Modes of Professionalization in Family Firms." *Family Business Review* 25, no. 1 (March 2012).

Strike, Vanessa M. "Advising the Family Firm: Reviewing the Past to Build the Future." *Family Business Review* 25, no. 2 (June 2012).

About the Website

Drawing on its rich tradition of incorporating research and practice in the family enterprise field, the Family Firm Institute has designed a companion website offering readers practical applications to extend and enhance their knowledge of the concepts covered in this book. The website contains interactive online learning features including self-assessment tools, actual case study applications, and downloadable readings. With its cutting-edge content and dynamic online platform, *Family Enterprise: Understanding Families in Business and Families of Wealth,* represents a new paradigm for applied learning in the field of family enterprise. We hope you enjoy the extended content at www.familyenterprisebook.com.

About FFI

The mission of the Family Firm Institute is to educate, connect, and inspire family enterprise consultants, academics, and other professionals, as well as organizations that support family enterprises.

Professionals, educators, and researchers as well as family business owners from more than 88 countries across the globe (almost half of all nations) belong to FFI. Together they create the oldest and most prestigious multidisciplinary professional association for family enterprise in the world.

About the Authors

Judy L. Green, PhD, is president of the Family Firm Institute. A published author and frequent presenter on the history of the family enterprise field and the evolution of the professional family enterprise advisor, she holds a PhD from Marquette University. The recipient of the prestigious Barbara Hollander Award, named for the founder of FFI, Ms. Green is also the technical editor of *The Complete Idiot's Guide to Successful Family Business* (Alpha Books/The Penguin Group, 2009).

Jane Hilburt-Davis, MSW, CAGS, ACFBA, is chair emeritus of the Family Firm Institute and developed the curriculum for FFI's Global Education Network (GEN). The co-author of the best-selling book *Consulting to Family Businesses*, Ms. Hilburt-Davis is the president of Key Resources and in 2008 received the FFI Richard Beckhard Practice Award.

Index

NOTE: Page references in *italics* refer to figures and tables.

accidental teams, 102, 145. *See also* multidisciplinary teamwork
advisors. *See* family business advisors
aligning/alignment, 82, 145
ambidexterity, of family enterprise, 25, 27
assessment, of needs, 71
Assessment Tests
   classic system, 43–44
   concepts of family enterprise, 77–79
   core professions used by family enterprise, 99–100
   family enterprise, generally, 37–38
   governance system, 50–51
   key characteristics of family enterprise, 57–58
   multidisciplinary teamwork, 138–139
   theoretical frameworks, 89–91
attitudes, of families, 15–19. *See also* family entrepreneurial orientation (FEO)
authority, 56, 145
avoidance orientation
   defined, 111
   as dimension of goal orientation, 105, 109–113
   discussion and conclusion, 124–132, *125*, *126*, *129*
   method, 113–116
   results, 116–124, *117*, *119*, *120–123*
   See also "Effects of Goal Orientation and Client Feedback on the Adaptive Behaviors of Family Enterprise Advisors, The" (Davis, Dibrell, Craig, Green)

balance point model, 81, 82, 83, 88–89, 145
basal system of economic activity, families as, 13
behavioral science professionals, 93, 94–98. *See also* multidisciplinary teamwork
board of advisors, 47, 145
board of directors, 47, 145–146
boundaries, 63, 146
Business Week, 53

case studies, 141–143
certified public accountants (CPA), 68

INDEX

change
  change process, 72–76
  patterns of, 75–76
  resistance to, 74–75
characteristics of family enterprise. *See* family enterprise characteristics
classic system, 39–44
  Assessment Test, 43–44
  enterprise system, 39–40, 42
  family system, 39–41
  ownership system, 39–40, 41–42
  theoretical frameworks and, 84–85
clients, defined, 146
closed systems, 60
closure, of businesses, 12
collaborative teams, 101, 146. *See also* multidisciplinary teamwork
commitment, as family enterprise characteristic, 54
communication management process, 69–72
competitiveness, as family enterprise characteristic, 54
conflict resolution, 64, 68, 72
consultants. *See* family business consultants (FBC)
content, defined, 63, 150. *See also* process and content
contingency theory, 19
controlling ownership, 87, 146
core disciplines of family enterprise professionals, 93–100
  Assessment Test, 99–100
  behavioral science professionals, 93, 94–95
  defined, 146
  financial professionals, 93, 94
  legal professionals, 93–94
  management science professionals, 93, 94
  perceptual filters and, 95–96
corporate strategy, family level of analysis an, 10
cousin consortium, developmental model and, 87, 147
customers, as external stakeholders, 85–86

Davis, Walter D., 103–138
decision-making rights
  family as stakeholder and, 9
  family enterprise, defined, 2–3
developmental model, 81, 82, 87, 147
Dibrell, Clay, 103–138
directors, board of, 47, 145–146
divestment, of businesses, 12
double bind, 69–70
dysfunctional teams, 102, 147. *See also* multidisciplinary teamwork

economic ventures, family enterprise as, 2, 3
"Effects of Goal Orientation and Client Feedback on the Adaptive Behaviors of Family Enterprise Advisors, The" (Davis, Dibrell, Craig, Green), 103–138
  discussion and conclusion, 124–132, *125, 126, 129*
  impact of goal orientation of family enterprise advisors on client feedback and advisor adaptive behaviors, *106*

introduction, 104–106
literature review and hypothesis development, 106–113
method, 113–116
results, 116–124, *117, 119, 120–123*
enterprise governance, 46–47
enterprise groups, 2, 3
enterprise system
　defined, 39–40, 42
　three-circle model and, 84, 85
entrepreuneurial activity
　of controlling family, *16–17*
　entrepreneur, defined, 147
　study of, 5
　transgenerational entrepreneurship research framework, 7
estate planners, 97, 147
European Union, 3
evaluation, *56*, 147
executive coaches, 97, 147
"Expert Group, Overview of Family-Business-Relevant Issues: Research, Networks, Policy Measures and Existing Studies" (European Union), 3
expert opinion, 70–71
external stakeholders, 85–86

family business, defined, 147
family business advisors
　behavioral science professionals, 93, 94–95
　board of, 47, 145
　consultants *versus*, 96–98
　defined, 40, 145, 148
　as external stakeholders, 85–86
　financial professionals, 93, 94
　legal professionals, 93–94
　management science professionals, 93, 94
　personne de confiance, 150
　as team members, 110–112 (*See also* multidisciplinary teamwork)
　trusted advisors, 98, 152
　types of multidisciplinary teams, 101–102 (*See also* multidisciplinary teamwork)
family business consultants (FBC)
　advisors *versus*, 96–98
　consulting firms, 101, 146 (*See also* multidisciplinary teamwork)
　defined, 68, 146
　family business consultants (FBC), 68
Family Business Review, 3, 4–37, 103, 153–154. *See also* "Effects of Goal Orientation and Client Feedback on the Adaptive Behaviors of Family Enterprise Advisors, The" (Davis, Dibrell, Craig, Green); "From Longevity of Firms to Transgenerational Entrepreneurship of Families: Introducing Family Entrepreneurial Orientation" (Zellweger, Nason, Nordqvist); "Using the Process/Content Framework: Guidelines for the Content Expert" (Hilburt-Davis, Senturia)

family council, 47–48
family dynamics
  family systems compared to enterprise systems, 55–57, 56
  governance systems and, 54–55
  See also family enterprise characteristics
family enterprise, generally, 1–38
  Assessment Test, 37–38
  case studies, 141–143
  defined, 1–3, 11, 148
  "From Longevity of Firms to Transgenerational Entrepreneurship of Families: Introducing Family Entrepreneurial Orientation" (Zellweger, Nason, Nordqvist), 4–37
  professionals hired by, 93–100
  See also family enterprise characteristics; family enterprise concepts
family enterprise characteristics, 53–58
  Assessment Test, 57–58
  challenges of, 54–55
  family systems compared to enterprise systems, 55–57, 56
  generally, 53–54
family enterprise concepts, 59–79
  Assessment Test, 77–79
  process and content, defined, 59, 63–65
  process and content, "Using the Process/Content Framework: Guidelines for the Content Expert" (Hilburt-Davis, Senturia), 65–76
  system theory, 59, 60, 61–63

family entrepreneurial orientation (FEO)
  defined, 24
  entrepreunuerial activity of controlling family, 16–17
  family-related business activity and, 23
  future directions, 27
  generally, 6, 15–19
  paradoxical thinking for, 25
  scale-building and, 20–23, 21–22, 26
Family Firm Institute
  Family Business Review, 3, 103, 153–154
  mission of, 157
  "2007 American Family Business Survey," 98
  website of, 155
  See also "Effects of Goal Orientation and Client Feedback on the Adaptive Behaviors of Family Enterprise Advisors, The" (Davis, Dibrell, Craig, Green); "From Longevity of Firms to Transgenerational Entrepreneurship of Families: Introducing Family Entrepreneurial Orientation" (Zellweger, Nason, Nordqvist); "Using the Process/Content Framework: Guidelines for the Content Expert" (Hilburt-Davis, Senturia)
family involvement in ownership (FIO), 2, 3
family level of analysis
  consequences, 10–13

generally, 7–10
See also "From Longevity of Firms to Transgenerational Entrepreneurship of Families: Introducing Family Entrepreneurial Orientation" (Zellweger, Nason, Nordqvist)
family system
  defined, 39–41, 148
  family-systems theory, generally, 67
  three-circle model and, 84
family therapy systems movement, 59
feedback quality
  avoidance orientation and, 112, *126,* 127
  defined, 106, 108
  feedback environment scale, 115
  importance of, 128, 131
  learning orientation and, 110, 111, 124, *126*
  proving orientation and, 112, 113, 124, *126*
  See also "Effects of Goal Orientation and Client Feedback on the Adaptive Behaviors of Family Enterprise Advisors, The" (Davis, Dibrell, Craig, Green)
financial professionals, 93, 94, 95–98, 148. *See also* multidisciplinary teamwork
firm-level studies, 8, 17. *See also* family level of analysis
formal systems, 148
Fortune 500 companies (publicly traded), family controlled, 12

foundations, 42, 148
founders, 41, 46, 149
"From Longevity of Firms to Transgenerational Entrepreneurship of Families: Introducing Family Entrepreneurial Orientation" (Zellweger, Nason, Nordqvist), 3, 4–37
  conclusion, 28
  discussion, 23–25
  exploratory findings, 13
  family entrepreneurial orientation (FEO), generally, 6, 15–19
  family entrepreneurial orientation (FEO), results, 20–23, *21–22*
  family level of analysis, consequences, 10–13
  family level of analysis, generally, 7–10
  implications for practice, 28
  intrafamily business succession, 4–6
  limitations and future research, 25–27
  method, 14–15
  results, 15, *16–17*
  transgenerational entrepreneurship research framework, 7

gender, family enterprise concepts and, 66
goal orientation. *See* "Effects of Goal Orientation and Client Feedback on the Adaptive Behaviors of Family Enterprise Advisors, The" (Davis, Dibrell, Craig, Green)

governance system, 45–52
  Assessment Test, 50–51
  defined, 45–46, 149
  enterprise governance, 46–47
  family council, 47–48
  ownership forums, 49–50
  three-circle model and, 85
Green, Judy, 103–138

Hilburt-Davis, Jane, 65–76
homeostasis, 62–63, 149

individual innovative behavior
  defined, 104, 106, *106*, 107–108
  learning orientation and, 110
  measures, *117*, 118
  personal bricolage and, 116
  results, *119*, *120–123*, 124, 126–128, *127*
  See also "Effects of Goal Orientation and Client Feedback on the Adaptive Behaviors of Family Enterprise Advisors, The" (Davis, Dibrell, Craig, Green)
individuals, within theoretical frameworks, 85, 86
informal systems, 149
innovativeness, as family enterprise characteristic, 54
interdependence
  balance point model and, 88–89
  defined, 149
interpersonal relationships, between family members. *See* family dynamics
intrafirm succession approach
  family enterprise concepts and, 64–65

longevity of family firms *versus*, 5
resistance toward, 55
succession planning, defined, 151

Journal of Finance, The, 53

Kennesaw State University, 98
key characteristics of family enterprise. *See* family enterprise characteristics

learning orientation
  conclusion, *126*, 126–130, *129*
  defined, 109
  as dimension of goal orientation, 105, 109–113
  hypotheses, 118–119, *119*, *120–123*, 124
  measures, 114
  results, 116, *117*, 118
  See also "Effects of Goal Orientation and Client Feedback on the Adaptive Behaviors of Family Enterprise Advisors, The" (Davis, Dibrell, Craig, Green)
legacy, as family enterprise characteristic, 54
legal professionals, 93–94, 95–98, 149. *See also* multidisciplinary teamwork
legal structure, 149
legal system, 149–150
longevity, of family enterprise
  "From Longevity of Firms to Transgenerational Entrepreneurship of Families: Introducing Family

Entrepreneurial Orientation"
(Zellweger, Nason, Nordqvist), 3
key characteristics and, 53–54
loyalty, as family enterprise
characteristic, 53

management
input from family members not
in management, 55
management science
professionals, 93, 94, 95–98,
150 (*See also* multidisciplinary
teamwork)
See also owners
MassMutual, 98
multidisciplinary teamwork,
101–139
Assessment Test, 138–139
challenges of, 102–103
generally, 101
multidisciplinary teams, defined,
150
"The Effects of Goal Orientation
and Client Feedback on the
Adaptive Behaviors of Family
Enterprise Advisors" (Davis,
Dibrell, Craig, Green), 103–
138
types of, 101–102
multigenerational families,
104, 150

Nason, Robert S., 3, 4–37
needs assessment, 71
negotiation, 64, 68
nimbleness, as family enterprise
characteristic, 54
nonverbal cues, 64
Nordqvist, Mattias, 3, 4–37

open systems, 60
optimism, as family enterprise
characteristic, 53
owners
controlling ownership, 87, 146
founders, 41, 46, 149
multiple members of same family
as, 2, 3
ownership groups, 150
ownership forum, 49–50, 150
ownership system
defined, 39–40, 41–42, 150
three-circle model and, 84

paradox perspective, 19, 25
partnership, 46, 150
perception filters, 95–96, 150
personal bricolage
defined, 104, 106, *106*, 107–108
individual innovative behavior
and, 116
learning orientation and, 110,
111, 113
measures, 115, *117*, 118
results, *119*, *120–123*, 124,
126–128, *127*
See also "Effects of Goal
Orientation and Client Feedback
on the Adaptive Behaviors of
Family Enterprise Advisors, The"
(Davis, Dibrell, Craig, Green)
personne de confiance, 150
primogeniture custom, 55
process and content
defined, 63, 67, 150
"Using the Process/Content
Framework: Guidelines for
the Content Expert" (Hilburt-
Davis, Senturia), 65–76

process and content, defined, 59, 63–65
proving orientation
　defined, 111
　as dimension of goal orientation, 105, 109–113
　discussion and conclusion, 124–132, *125, 126, 129*
　method, 113–116
　results, 116–124, *117, 119, 120–123*
　See also "Effects of Goal Orientation and Client Feedback on the Adaptive Behaviors of Family Enterprise Advisors, The" (Davis, Dibrell, Craig, Green)

readings, suggested, 153–154
relationships, between family members. See family dynamics
representative governance systems (governance systems?)
　theoretical frameworks and, 84–85
risk and innovation orientation, 24–25

"safety zones," creating, 73–74
scale building, family entrepreneurial orientation (FEO) and, 20–23, *21–22,* 26
scapegoating, 62, 150
Senturia, Peg, 65–76
separation, balance point model and, 88–89
share capital, 3
shareholders
　family system and, 41

governance system and, 47
sibling partnership, 87, 151
S&P 500 companies, family firms as, 53
stakeholders
　defined, 151
　external, 85–86
　family as, 8–9
　stewardship, 151
succession
　family enterprise concepts and, 64–65
　longevity of family firms *versus,* 5
　resistance toward, 55
　succession planning, defined, 151
suppliers, as external stakeholders, 85–86
system, defined, 151
system dynamics, 151
systems theory, 59, 60, 61–63, 151

teams, multidisciplinary. See multidisciplinary teamwork
theoretical frameworks, 81–91
　Assessment Test, 89–91
　balance point model, 81, 82, 83, 88–89
　developmental model, 81, 82, 87
　three-circle model, 81, 83–86
third parties, triangling and, 61–62
three-circle model
　consultants and, 97–98
　defined, 81, 83–86, 151
transgenerational entrepreneurship research framework, 7
transgenerational value creation
　defined, 4, 5
　growth expectancy and, 27
　implications of, 28

internal and external autonomy, 18
transgenerational entrepreneurship, defined, 6–7
transgenerational entrepreneurship research framework, 7
See also "From Longevity of Firms to Transgenerational Entrepreneurship of Families: Introducing Family Entrepreneurial Orientation" (Zellweger, Nason, Nordqvist)
transition, 151–152
triangling (triangulation), 61–62, 152
trusted advisors, 98, 152
"2007 American Family Business Survey" (MassMutual, Kennesaw State University, Family Firm Institute), 98

unitary actors, families as, 12–13

"Using the Process/Content Framework: Guidelines for the Content Expert" (Hilburt-Davis, Senturia), 65–76
change process, 72–76
communication management process, 69–72
integrating process and content in consultation, 68–69
introduction, 65–68

valuation, 152
values, 152
vigilance, as family enterprise characteristic, 54
vision, family business governed/managed with, 2, 3

Ward, John, 4, 11–12, 26
wealth, transgenerational entrepreneurship and, 12

Zellweger, Thomas Markus, 3, 4–37